Let my

temptation

be a book

t

Making 75 Rugs by the Square

ALSO BY DAVID P. BLAKE AND CHARLES BARNES

Bargello and Related Stitchery
Macramé Fashions and Furnishings
120 Needlepoint Design Projects

Making 75 Rugs by the Square

Rugs to Work in
Latchet Hook, Rya,
Punch, and Gros Point

David P. Blake,
Charles Barnes,
& Charles Thompson

Crown Publishers, Inc.
New York

ACKNOWLEDGMENTS

We would like to express our gratitude to Emil Bernat & Sons for their enthusiastic cooperation in the preparation of this book. Their generous contribution of the finest quality Rya Rug Yarn, Quickspun Rug Yarn, Craftsman Rug Yarn, Tabriz Needleart Yarn, and rug canvas enabled us to explore many creative approaches to rugmaking which would have otherwise been denied us.

Printed in the United States of America
Published simultaneously in Canada by
General Publishing Company Limited

Design by Jon M. Nelson

Library of Congress Cataloging in Publication Data

Blake, David P
  Making 75 rugs by the square.

  Includes index.
  1. Rugs. I. Barnes, Charles, joint author.
II. Thompson, Charles, 1939– joint author.
III. Title.
TT850.B52 1978   746.7'4   77-10718
ISBN 0-517-52471-6
ISBN 0-517-52472-4 pbk.

Contents

Introduction

Creating a rug can be a stimulating and rewarding project—whether it be a small area rug designed to serve as a decorative accent or a larger room-sized rug whose purpose is to serve as a unifying color and design factor. However, you may be deterred from undertaking such a large project. This book offers one practical solution to this problem, namely, work your rug in small squares. Sew the squares together, and before you know it you have completed your rug, whether small area size or giant room size. The seventy-five designs range from traditional to modern to whimsical and may be worked in flat stitches, latchet, punch, or rya. A single design may be repeated in the same color, repeated in different color combinations, or repeated in different stitch techniques. And, of course, the number of different designs that can be combined in your rug will be limited only by your decorative needs and your imagination.

Materials and Methods

YARN

Do not skimp on the quality of yarn just to save a few pennies. The yarn is the material that comes into direct contact with the traffic and suffers the wear and tear. Therefore, you should not jeopardize the life expectancy of your rug by selecting an inferior yarn.

Make sure the yarn is colorfast. If it is not, the colors may run together during blocking and ruin your rug. Also, yarns that are not colorfast tend to fade quickly or lose color when cleaned.

Wool yarns, or yarns made of a wool and synthetic fiber combination, are to be preferred above all others. Yarns made entirely of synthetic fibers are generally satisfactory. Our experience leads us to the conclusion that yarns made from a cotton and rayon combination are unsatisfactory since they do not wear well. Yarn to be used for flat stitches should have long, even fibers and should be full enough to completely cover the canvas.

The amount of yarn required for each square will be determined by your own stitching technique and the type of stitches employed. To determine the amount you will need for a project, measure a specific amount of each color. Work one square. Subtract the amount of yarn you have left from the amount you started with. This will give you an approximation of how much of each color you need for one square. Multiply the amount of each color you used times the number of squares you plan to make for the whole rug. Purchase, or at least lay away, the entire amount of yarn you will need, making sure it all comes from the same dye lot. Shades may vary considerably from one dye lot to another.

1

Plate 1. This assortment of yarns includes all the types used for the projects throughout this book. The cut skein at the left and the two uncut skeins at the upper right are used for flat stitches. The skein in the center is used for punch. The packaged skein at the lower right front is for rya and the shorter packaged skein above it is for latchet.

Yarn that is used for flat stitches is sold in skeins. Carefully open each skein so you have a large loop of yarn. Cut the skein at each end of the loop. Latchet and rya yarns are generally available in precut packages. Punch yarns are available in skeins, as is the yarn sold for flat stitches, or in pull skeins. In either case, do not cut the yarn into short lengths. If you are using a pull skein, just pull the yarn out of the skein as you use it. If the yarn is not wound in a pull skein, cut one strand of yarn and roll it into a ball.

COLOR SELECTION

Color combinations indicated in the charts are only some of an unlimited number of possibilities. You should feel free to change individual colors or select entirely new combinations to meet your specific needs. Your selection should be guided by a few considerations.

If you are planning an area rug or wall hanging that is to be a focal point in the room, your color selection can be more dramatic than if you are planning a large, room-size rug. While the colors should be coordinated with the other furnishings, you should choose stronger and more intense shades than those used throughout the room. This would also apply if you are using individual squares as accent pillows.

If possible, choose all your colors at one time. Lay the colors out, side by side. If one color looks discordant, substitute another for it. Remember, also, that full skeins of yarn will look much brighter than when they are worked up into stitches.

If you are making a large room-size or very important area rug, you may want to work one square before purchasing all your yarn. If the selection is not exactly what you want you can always use the square as an accent pillow or in another room.

CANVAS AND BURLAP

The backing fabric for your rug will be canvas or burlap. It should be of the highest quality, the threads being evenly spaced and free from knots.

Canvas threads should have a smooth glaze, indicating that they have been properly treated to retain their position. The glaze will also facilitate the passage of the yarn through the holes when working flat stitches. Individual canvas and burlap threads should be strong. If you can break one easily they may break just as easily during blocking and will probably not wear as long as they should.

Rug canvas is referred to as having four or five mesh. This means that there are either four or five pairs of threads per inch. Latchet and rya are worked on four-mesh canvas. Punch may be worked on five-mesh canvas or burlap. If the punch needle does not pass easily through the five-mesh canvas, carefully squeeze the flanged edges of the needle together. You may also crumple the canvas thoroughly to accommodate the punch needle. Burlap is usually woven ten or twelve threads per inch, with the twelve being preferred. Flat stitches are worked on either four- or five-mesh canvas.

Plate 2. The square at the lower right is burlap for punch; the square at the center left is 5-mesh canvas for punch or flat stitches; and the square at the back is 4-mesh canvas for latchet or rya.

DETERMINING THE SIZE OF EACH SQUARE

The size of each square will depend upon the mesh of the canvas or burlap you use for backing fabric. To ascertain the size each square will be when worked on four-mesh canvas, for flat stitches, latchet, or rya, count the number of squares across the chart. Divide this number by four and you will have the number of inches the design will measure across. Do the same with the vertical squares and you will have the height of the design. To determine the size of each square when worked with flat stitches or punch on five-mesh canvas, divide the number of squares by five. If you plan to punch the design on burlap, refer to the section entitled "Transferring Designs to Burlap." Designs having no background indicated on the chart, such as the Key on Broken Cane, Plate 46, may be worked on any size square that is large enough to accommodate the design itself.

CANVAS AND BURLAP MARGINS

After selecting the designs you wish to work, decide on the technique and type of canvas or burlap you will need. Each canvas or burlap square must be cut at least four inches larger than the background area. If you are working on canvas make sure that you cut each square from the canvas in the same direction. The woven edges of the canvas should always be on the sides. This is very important because the threads may not be woven exactly the same number to the inch, both vertically and horizontally. Thus, a piece of canvas with fifty vertical pairs of threads and fifty horizontal pairs of threads may not be exactly square. To save confusion later on, mark the top of each square when you cut it.

The cut edges of canvas and burlap unravel with alarming ease. One easy method of dealing with this problem is to cover the cut edges with masking tape. Cut a piece of one- or two-inch-wide tape the length of one side of the square. Press half the tape, lengthwise, on the top side of the canvas or burlap. Fold the tape over the raw edge and press on the back. Repeat on all sides. Leave the tape on the canvas or burlap until you are ready to sew the pieces together.

TRANSLATING CHARTS TO CANVAS

All designs have been charted on graph paper enabling you to exactly duplicate the sample shown in each photograph. When working graphic designs or designs having a definite center you will probably find it easier to start from the center of the chart and work to the outside edge of the square. Examples of this type of design are Interlocking Bands, Plate 12; Byzantine Square, Plate 17; Leaf Stitch Center, Plate 19; and Stained Glass, Plate 35. When working designs containing a specific subject, you will probably find it easier to begin at a specific point on the design and work the complete design before proceeding to the background area. Some of these designs include Giant Persian, Plate 27; Tree of Life Quilt Design, Plate 33; and Aztec Priest, Plate 39.

Each square on the graph represents a different portion of the canvas for flat stitches, latchet and rya, or punch. For flat stitches each square on the chart represents the area where the two vertical and the two horizontal threads cross (Fig. 1). For a small stitch, such as the Continental, Fig. 173, each square represents one stitch. A larger stitch, such as the Mosaic, Fig. 192, would cover four squares. For latchet and rya each square on the chart represents the two horizontal threads between the intersection of the horizontal and vertical threads (Fig. 2). Each square is one latchet or rya stitch. When punch is worked on five-mesh canvas, each square represents one large hole on the canvas and is equal to one stitch (Fig. 3). Keeping these distinctions in mind, cover the canvas with stitches corresponding to the colors and stitches indicated on the charts. Instructions on how to translate the chart to burlap for punch are contained in the section entitled "Transferring Designs to Burlap."

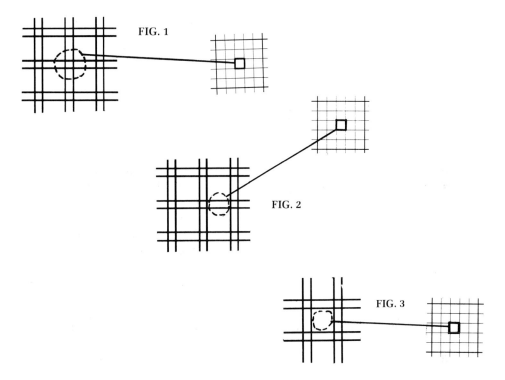

FIG. 1

FIG. 2

FIG. 3

PAINTING CANVAS

Rather than refer to the chart every time you make a stitch, you may find it easier to paint the entire canvas with the colors before beginning the actual work. If you choose this approach, be sure to remember that each square on the chart represents a different area of the canvas, depending upon the technique you decide to use.

Several types of coloring medium are available. Artist oils or acrylic paints are the best. You have a wide range of colors available and both are permanent when dry. The main disadvantages to oil-base paints are that they take a considerable amount of time to dry and are difficult to clean up. Also, most of the chemicals used to dilute them have strong, offensive odors. On the other hand, acrylics are diluted with water and so they dry quickly, have little or no odor, and can be cleaned up with soap and cold water. Whichever you use, they should be diluted to the consistency of cream. Apply them sparingly with an artist's brush and allow them to dry completely before beginning work. If you accidentally apply too much paint and the canvas becomes limp, pulling out of shape, stop painting. Spread the canvas out straight and allow to dry completely before continuing with the painting.

It is with some reservations that we recommend felt-tip pens. Even though many brands specify that they are completely waterproof when dry, our experience has been that once in a while one of the colors will run during blocking, ruining an entire design. If you wish to try them, however, test each tube before using it. To do this, cut a two-inch square of canvas and carefully mark several of the threads. After the square has dried completely, drop it into a clear glass of cold water. Remove the canvas and let it dry thoroughly. If the water discolors, or the color spreads on the canvas, do not use that tube. Be sure to test each tube.

TRANSFERRING DESIGNS TO BURLAP

Unlike canvas threads, which are woven straight across and up and down with a specific number of threads per inch, burlap threads are not woven as straight and usually vary in number from one inch to the next. Therefore, the design must be enlarged and physically transferred to the burlap.

Count the number of squares across the chart. Divide the number of squares by the number of inches you want your finished square to be. For example, if the chart has 100 squares across, and you want the finished square to be ten inches across, divide the 100 squares by ten. This will mean you need graph paper with ten squares per linear inch for enlarging your design. Copy the chart onto your 10-square graph paper. This will give you a new copy of the design exactly the size you want for your finished square. Place the new design on the burlap with dressmaker's carbon between. Make sure the carbon has the correct side facing the burlap. Pin the pattern to the burlap and trace the design, transferring it to the burlap. Check frequently to make sure that the design is transferring clearly. There are special tracing wheels available in most variety, art needlework, and department stores to facilitate the transfer. For larger, curved designs such as the Giant Sunflower, Plate 5; Giant Flower, Plate 30; and Japanese Girl, Plate 50, it is not necessary to mark out each square. Just follow the general outline of the design. Designs containing smaller, symmetrical elements will require a closer adherence to the squares. Examples of this type design are Interlocking Bands, Plate 12, and Florentine Tile, Plate 45.

FRAMES

Frames are necessary for work done in the punch stitch. Since the needle is repeatedly pushed through the canvas or burlap you must stretch the backing fabric securely to a frame. The frame should be sturdy and large enough so that the entire area to be punched is inside the inner edge of the frame. For punch, a frame with four sides to which the burlap or canvas can be secured is preferable to a rolling type. Otherwise the backing fabric may stretch out of shape along the edges. With flat stitches a frame is very helpful, and in some cases a necessity. The frame will hold the canvas in its original square shape, minimizing distortion. The need for blocking will be greatly reduced, or completely eliminated. For designs incorporating stitches that slant in opposite directions, such as Mosaic Nos. 1 and 2, Figs. 192 and 193, a frame is essential. The opposing tension of these stitches causes the canvas to peak, or form a point in the center of the square. If stitches are pulled too tight it may be impossible to block the square in order to completely remove the peak in the center. You may find it difficult to learn to work on a frame, but the extra effort is well worth it because of the superior piece of needlepoint you will make.

Latchet and rya need no frame, and, as a matter of fact, cannot be worked satisfactorily on a frame.

Plate 3. Illustrated here are a standing frame in the back, a rolling frame at the right, and a frame of artist stretchers at the left. Canvas has been taped and placed on a frame of artist stretchers at the bottom center of the picture; in the left front is a bare frame of artist stretchers. Standing frame courtesy of Design Point Needlepoint.

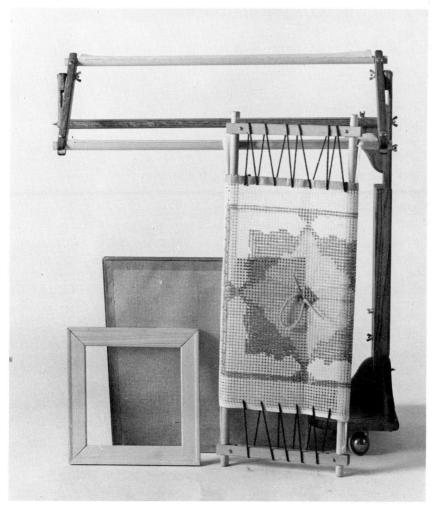

COMBINING DIFFERENT DESIGNS

Many interesting rugs can be made by combining different design squares (see Plates 36 and 47). However, you should keep several considerations in mind.

First, are the designs compatible in nature? If they are too dissimilar in style they may conflict with one another and detract from the total rug design. For example, a bold graphic such as the Graphic V, Plate 58, would not coordinate well with Tile Number One, Plate 6. They are just too dissimilar in design. One easy way to see if specific designs will work together is to make several tracings or photostats of the designs. Cut them into squares and place the different designs together. This way you can experiment with the number and placement of the designs before actually beginning the rug.

The second consideration should be, are the designs similar in size? Do not try to combine a square with a large design, such as the Giant Butterfly, Plate 69, with a small design such as the Bee, Plate 71.

After choosing several designs that you feel are compatible stylistically, refer to the charts and count the number of squares across and up and down the design. Do not include the background area. If the number of squares does not vary greatly, consider using them together. The background area may have to be altered from that shown on the charts. Either increase or reduce the size, remembering that all squares must be the same size when finished.

A third consideration should be the colors used in each of the different designs. To create a harmonious whole all the squares should have similar, or at least complementary, color schemes. If the colors indicated on the charts do not harmonize, by all means try a combination that suits your needs and enhances the design squares you have selected.

MAKING YOUR RUG IN ONE PIECE

For smaller area rugs you may decide to work the entire rug on one piece of canvas or burlap. The one basic disadvantage is that you lose a certain amount of mobility. The size of the canvas or burlap you will be working on will make it difficult, if not impossible, for you to carry it with you on the bus or in the car, or to work on it at the beach, patio, or the like. However, the big advantage is that you eliminate the need to block and sew together all the individual squares when completed. Before deciding on this method, you should consider several technical requirements.

If the rug is to contain flat stitches it is imperative that you use a frame and do not pull the stitches too tight. If no frame is used, or the stitches are pulled too tight, the rug may become so distorted that it may be difficult if not impossible to block it properly. In addition, because of the size of the rug it may be difficult to find a large enough surface on which to block it. Flat stitches that are pulled too tight may cause the rug to eventually stretch out of shape, even after proper blocking. So, be sure to use a frame, and do not pull the stitches too tight.

A rug worked in punch must be worked on a frame. If you choose a standing, rolling frame be sure to tie the sides of the burlap or canvas to the sides of the frame to prevent stretching of the edges. If the rug is more than twenty-four inches across do not use a flat frame since you will not be able to work on the center easily. The canvas for latchet and rya must be laid out flat when you are hooking, so make sure you have a table large enough to accommodate you comfortably. The weight of a piece of canvas worked in latchet, and especially rya, can be considerable, You may find that a one-foot strip of finished latchet or rya at one end of the canvas is just too heavy and unmanageable.

The canvas or burlap should be large enough for the finished rug, plus at least a two-inch margin on all sides. The margin will be necessary for blocking and finishing off the outside edges.

Consider both the pros and cons of working the rug on one piece of canvas. If you have the room for a frame or feel you can handle the project in one piece, then by all means consider this alternate method of making your rug.

LATCHET AND RYA TECHNIQUE

The technique employed for latchet and rya is basically the same—only the length and number of strands of yarn used for each vary. Latchet yarn is hooked one strand at a time, whereas rya is hooked three strands at a time. Figures 4 through 9 show latchet yarn being hooked. Follow the same procedure for rya, except use three strands of yarn at the same time.

Fold one piece of yarn in half over the shank of the hook, just below the latchet. Remember—for rya, use three strands of yarn.

FIG. 4

Push the hook down through the first hole, under two horizontal threads, and up through the hole directly above.

FIG. 5

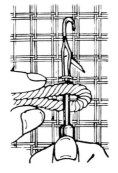

Draw the hook back toward you. Before the latchet closes, bring the two ends, which you have been holding in your left hand, over the shank of the hook between the latchet and hook.

FIG. 6

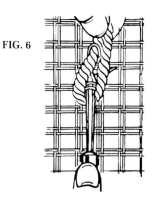

Draw the hook toward you until the latchet closes, then let go of the loose ends of yarn.

FIG. 7

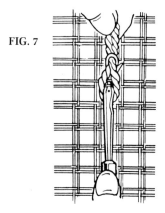

Draw the hook toward you until the loose ends of yarn have passed through the loop of yarn.

FIG. 8

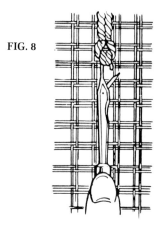

Tug both ends of yarn to tighten the knot.

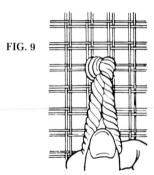

FIG. 9

FLAT STITCHES

The variety and number of flat stitches available to the rugmaker are almost limitless. They are basically needlepoint stitches that have been adapted to the larger mesh canvas commonly used for rugs. In many cases the basic needlepoint stitches have been reversed, making a completely symmetrical design possible. Examples of reversed stitches may be seen in the Continental Nos. 1 and 2, Figs. 173 and 174; Scotch Nos. 1 and 2, Figs. 177 and 178; and Byzantine Nos. 1 and 2, Figs. 194 and 195. Many of the larger stitches dictate the overall design itself, as in the designs Diamonds and Crosses, Plate 13; Byzantine Square, Plate 17; Leaf Stitch Center, Plate 19; and Graphic V, Plate 58. When you are working the larger patterned stitches, such as the Milanese, Fig. 180, and Byzantine, Fig. 194, you will often find it necessary to vary the stitch slightly to make it fit into the design area properly. On these occasions, shorten the length of each stitch, as necessary, but keep them slanting in the same direction as the whole stitch. A good example to note is the Giant Milanese, Plate 10. Complete diagrams of the flat stitches are shown in Figures 173 through 207.

Do not use knots when you begin or end a piece of yarn. They will cause bumps in your rug. When you begin each piece of yarn bring the rug needle up through the canvas but leave about one inch of yarn on the back of the canvas. With the first few stitches sew the yarn end to the back of the canvas. When you near the end of each piece of yarn weave it through the back of the last few stitches. Clip all tag ends of yarn off close to the back of the canvas.

PUNCH

Punch is probably the easiest and quickest of the techniques. Once the needle is threaded, the yarn is put in place with a simple "push-pull" motion. Thread the needle by inserting the yarn through the hole nearest the handle. Pull several inches of yarn through and slide it through the slot into the tube of the needle. Thread the yarn back out of the needle through the hole near the point. Make a knot in the end of the yarn and pull the knot against the needle. Begin by outlining one area of the design. Add parallel rows until the portion of the design is filled. Push the needle through the canvas or burlap until the handle touches the backing fabric. Pull the needle back up through the backing fabric, but do not

11

pull the point away from the backing fabric. If you are working on canvas, go down in the next hole. If you are working on burlap, make each stitch as close as possible to the preceding stitch.

FIG. 10

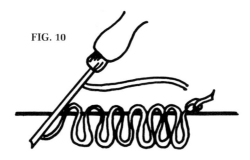

When you are finished with a color, pull several inches of yarn out of the needle. Cut the yarn and weave the tag end through the back of several stitches. Exercise caution with the completed areas because the yarn will pull out easily from the back.

COMBINING TECHNIQUES

Each design has several alternate stitch techniques suggested. Combining different techniques produces interesting textures and also makes the actual work more enjoyable. When combining techniques, keep the following suggestions in mind:

When combining latchet and rya, work each complete row of canvas, beginning with the side of canvas closest to you. Work each row of canvas until the entire square is covered. Do not skip any areas as it is very difficult to use the hook in an area surrounded with pieces of latchet or rya yarn.

When combining latchet or rya with flat stitches, work the flat stitches first; otherwise, the latchet or rya will spread out and be in your way when you try to work the flat stitches. Also, the latchet or rya yarn will get tangled with your flat stitches.

Punch may be successfully combined with flat stitches if both are worked on five-mesh rug canvas. Work the flat stitches first, or the punch will spread out and be in the way or tangle with the flat stitches. The canvas may be on or off a frame for the flat stitches. To work the punch, the canvas must be on a frame, and you must work from the reverse side. If punch is to be worked on burlap do not try to combine with flat stitches. Flat stitches cannot be worked satisfactorily on burlap. Our experience has been that punch does not cover four-mesh rug canvas properly. Therefore, we do not recommend combining latchet or rya with punch.

BLOCKING

Blocking is the process of returning a finished piece of canvas, which has become distorted during the stitching, to its original square shape. Flat stitches invariably distort the canvas, while latchet, punch, or rya rarely cause this problem. Using a frame while working flat stitches will usually minimize or completely eliminate the need for blocking. If stitches are pulled too tight, returning the canvas to its original square shape may be difficult, if not impossible.

You will need a piece of smooth plywood or composition board several inches larger than the canvas to be blocked. Cover the blocking board with several layers of clean brown wrapping paper or white drawing paper. Do not use newspaper or any paper with a design that may run when wet. Draw a square on the paper the same size as the outside measurement of the canvas.

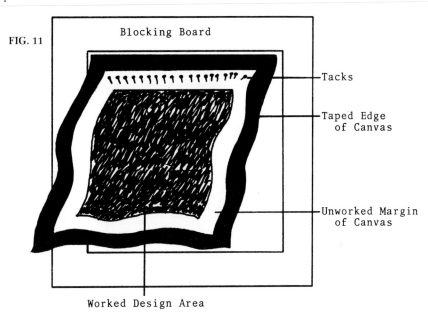

FIG. 11

Blocking Board

Tacks

Taped Edge of Canvas

Unworked Margin of Canvas

Worked Design Area

If the square is worked entirely in flat stitches, lay the canvas face down on the paper. If latchet, punch, or rya has been employed, leave the design face up. Using rustproof tacks, pushpins, or staples, tack or staple the top edge of the canvas to the top line. Drive the tacks, pushpins, or staples three-fourths of the way into the board. Place them close to the outside edge of the canvas, approximately one-half to one inch apart.

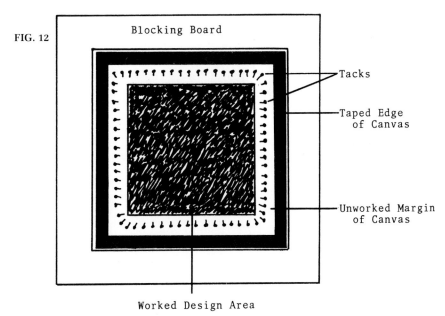

FIG. 12

Blocking Board

Tacks

Taped Edge of Canvas

Unworked Margin of Canvas

Worked Design Area

Pull one other side of the canvas to the pattern line and tack or staple it in place. Repeat this process with the two remaining sides. If you cannot pull the canvas completely square, pull it as close to the square pattern line as possible. Dampen the back of the canvas with water. Do not saturate. Lay the blocking board flat in a cool, dry place until the canvas is completely dry. Remove each tack or staple individually. If you could not block the canvas completely square the first time, repeat the process. As soon after blocking as possible, make the squares into a pillow or rug.

FINISHING AND JOINING SQUARES

After blocking each square, trim the canvas or burlap margin to within one inch of the finished area. Cut the corner margin off diagonally about one-half inch from the corner of the finished area.

FIG. 13

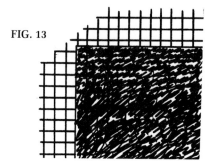

Turn the diagonally cut canvas or burlap to the back side of the finished area. The fold should come directly to the corner of the finished area.

FIG. 14

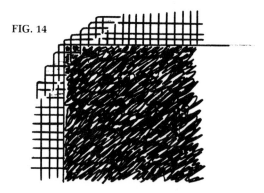

Turn one side of the canvas or burlap to the back side of the finished area. If the area along the margin has been worked in flat stitches it is essential that the fold be made right on the outside edge of the stitches so no canvas will be exposed.

FIG. 15

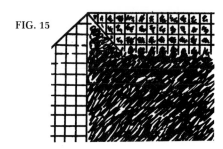

Repeat the procedure on all sides. Stitch the canvas margins together where they meet at each corner. Stitch the raw straight edges of the canvas to the back of the finished area. Stitches should include several canvas or burlap threads to keep them from unraveling.

FIG. 16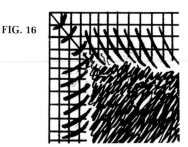

To join flat stitched squares together, turn the squares face up. Carefully match the rows of stitches on the adjoining squares. Sew the squares together, placing each sewing stitch between the needlepoint stitches so they do not show. If possible, use thread that matches the yarn color.

FIG. 17

For joining latchet, punch, or rya squares, use the same procedure, but lay the squares face down and sew from the back.

FINISHING THE COMPLETED RUG

After all squares have been sewn together finish off the outside edge with a binding tape. The tape should be wide enough to cover the raw canvas margin and its stitching. Use small, evenly placed stitches and sew the tape as close to the edge as possible, without its showing from the top.

FIG. 18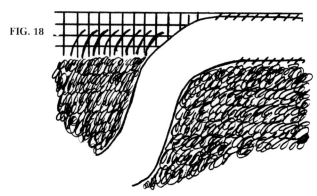

You do not need to back the whole rug with a lining. As a matter of fact, a lining may only serve to trap dirt between the back of the rug and the lining. Punch rugs are usually coated with a latex mixture made especially for this purpose. It keeps the loops from being accidentally pulled out and makes the rug nonskidding.

MAKING PILLOWS

You may decide to use individual design squares as pillows, either by themselves, or to coordinate with your rug. If the outside edge of the square is worked in flat stitches, block the square and trim the canvas margin to within one inch of the finished area. Cut a piece of backing fabric the same size as the outside edge of the canvas. Lay the backing fabric on a flat surface, face up. Lay the finished piece of needlepoint on top of the backing fabric, face down. Pin the two pieces together. Sew together, on top of the outside row of stitches, leaving six to eight inches open on one side. Turn the pillow inside out through the opening. After filling with stuffing, sew the opening closed. If the outside edge of the square is worked with latchet, punch, or rya, follow the instructions accompanying Figures 13 through 16. Cut a piece of backing fabric two inches larger than the canvas. Turn under a one-inch margin on all sides of the backing fabric. Place the rug square on a flat surface, face down. Lay the backing fabric on the back of the square, face up. Pin the two pieces together. Sew the backing to the canvas, leaving six to eight inches open on one side. After stuffing, sew this opening closed.

CARE AND CLEANING

A rug properly made with quality materials should last a lifetime, barring unnatural abuse or accidents. As with any other prized possession, your rug should be protected from the wear and tear of excessive traffic, dirt, and sunlight. For periodic cleaning, your rug should be entrusted to a reputable cleaner. Make sure he has proper equipment and cleaning solutions. Remember, one bad cleaning could ruin your rug, and no amount of compensation can replace your many long hours of loving work. Our experience has indicated that machine- or hand-washing is too abusive and damaging to handmade rugs.

Designs
for the
Whole House

The seventy-five designs have been divided into groups and have been placed in various rooms of the house. In many cases you will find other locations in your home for various designs. Our selection should not limit you, but is merely a suggestions as to one of many possible uses for each design.

For the Living Room

Plate 4. Tile Number 3 (see Fig. 39). This rug combines three techniques: flat stitches, latchet, and rya fringe. The flat stitches have been reversed in each square to add interest and to minimize the distortion that might have occurred if all the stitches had been worked in the same direction.

Giant Sunflower

Figs. 19, 20, and Plate 5

FIG. 19

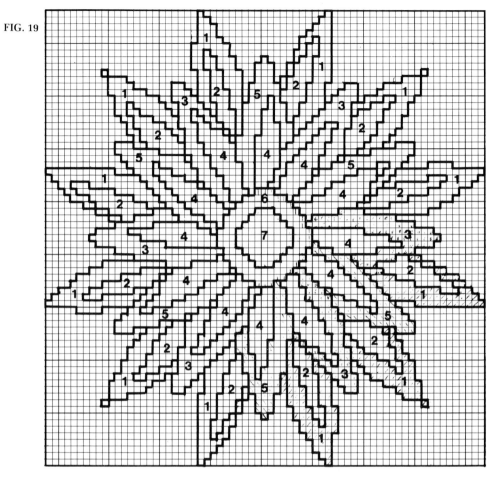

FIG. 20

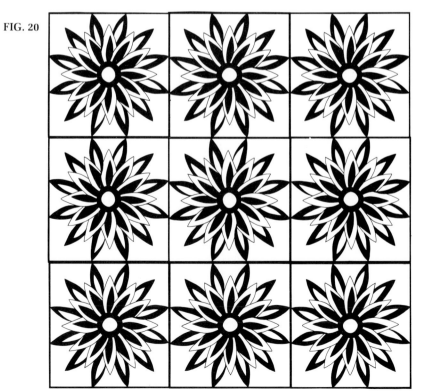

Plate 5. Giant Sunflower. Executed by Sue Jane Wentz.

Other Stitch Suggestions:

1. Work the entire square in latchet, punch, or rya.

2. Work the entire flower in latchet, punch, or rya and the background in fiat stitches.

Colors and Stitches:

1 Dark Gold Continental No. 1
2 Medium Gold Continental No. 1
3 Light Gold Continental No. 1

4 Light Yellow Continental No. 1
5 Medium Yellow Continental No. 1
6 Dark Orange Diagonal Mosaic No. 1
7 Light Orange Diagonal Mosaic No. 1
Background—Dark Brown Scotch No. 1

Tile Number One
Figs. 21, 22, and Plate 6

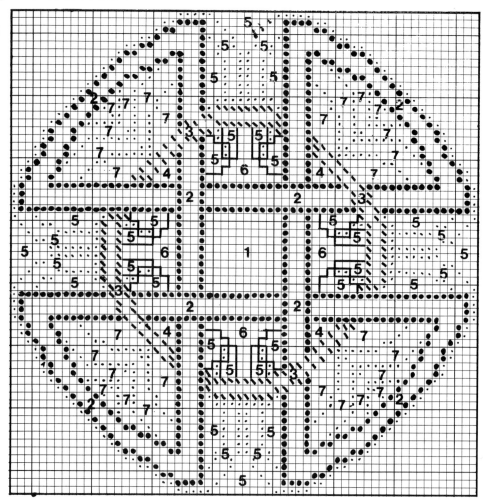

FIG. 21

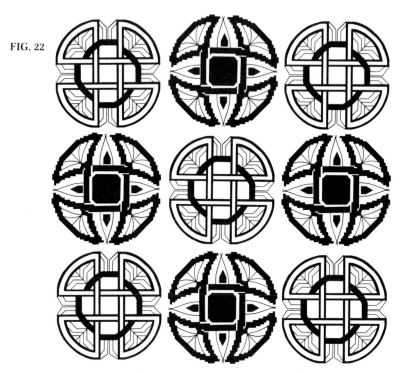

FIG. 22

Plate 6. Tile Number One.
Other Stitch Suggestions:
   1. Work the entire square in latchet or punch.
   2. Work the design circle in latchet or punch and the corners in flat stitches.

Colors and Stitches:

1   Alternating Dark Blue and Dark
    Purple Continental No. 1
2   One Row of Rust and One Row of
    Red Continental No. 1
3   Dark Pink Continental No. 1
4   Dark Blue Continental No. 1

5   Light Gray Continental No. 1
6   Grayish Purple Continental No. 1
7   Light Blue Continental No. 1
●   Light Pink Continental No. 1
/   Dark Pink Continental No. 1
●   Grayish Purple Continental No. 1
Background—Black Flat Stem No. 1

23

Tile Number Two
Figs. 23, 24, and Plate 7

FIG. 23

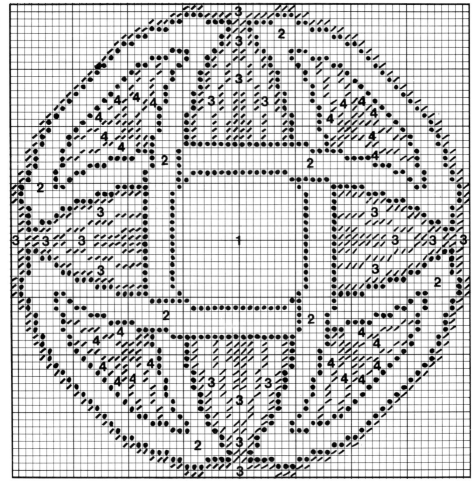

FIG. 24

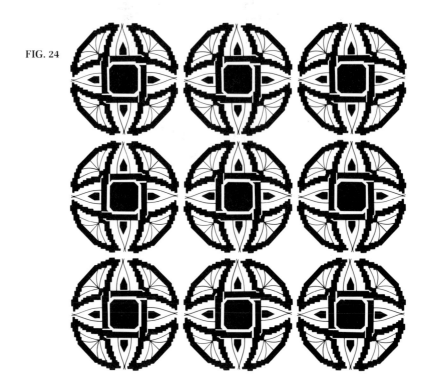

24

Plate 7. Tile Number Two.
  Other Stitch Suggestions:
    1. Work the entire square in latchet or punch.
    2. Work the design circle in latchet or punch and the corners in flat stitches.

Colors and Stitches:

1 Alternating Dark and Medium Purple Continental No. 1
2 Bright Rose Continental No. 1
3 Light Blue Continental No. 1
4 Light Gray Continental No. 1
● Pink Continental No. 1
\ Grayish Purple Continental No. 1
Background—Black Flat Stem No. 1

25

Giant Rose
Figs. 25, 26, and Plate 8

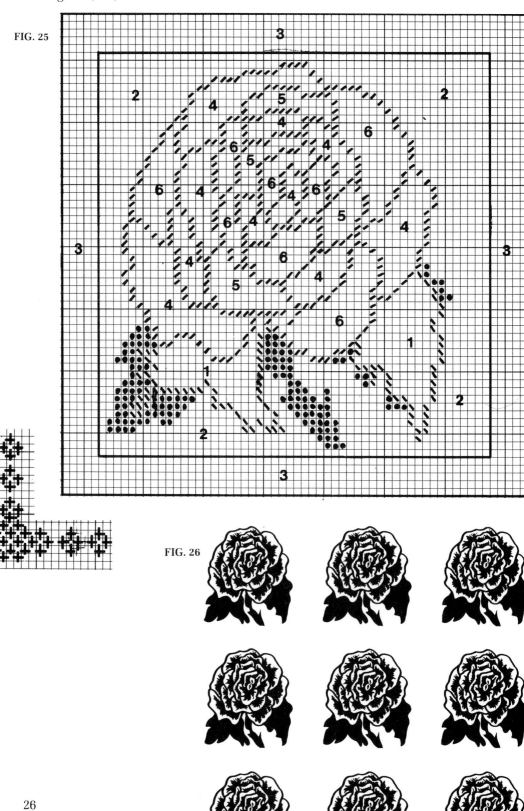

FIG. 25

FIG. 26

26

Plate 8. Giant Rose.
   Other Stitch Suggestions:
      1. Work the entire square in latchet or rya.
      2. Work the rose and leaves in latchet, punch, or rya and the background in flat stitches.

Colors and Flat Stitches:

1 Dark Green Continental No. 1
2 White Continental No. 1
3 Pink Straight Cross in Diamond Pattern and White Flat Stem Nos. 1, 2, 3, and 4 (see detail of border)
4, 5, and 6   Fill in rose with a random placement of Light and Medium Pink Diagonal Mosaic No. 1
/ Burgundy Continental No. 1
\ Dark Green Continental No. 1
● Light Green Continental No. 1

Punch Colors:

1 Dark Green
2 Dark Brown
3 and + Dark Gold and Brown in Diamond Pattern (see detail of border)
4 Medium Orange
5 Red
6 Light Orange
/ Medium Orange
\ Dark Green
● Light Green

Chinese Medallion
Figs. 27, 28, and Plate 9

FIG. 27

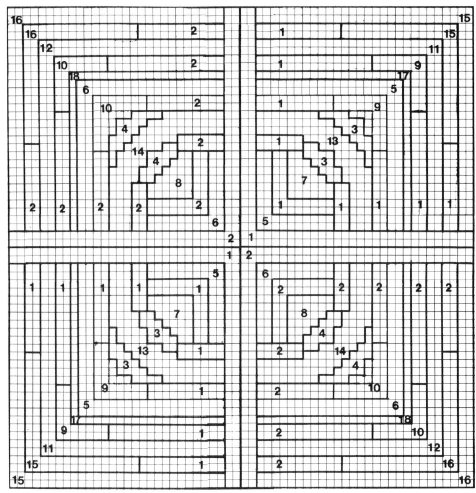

FIG. 28

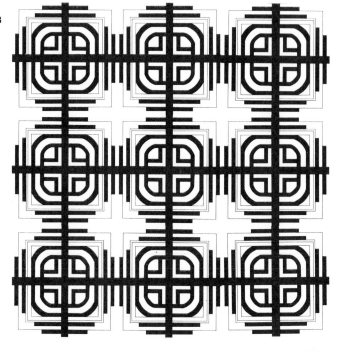

Plate 9. Chinese Medallion.
Other Stitch Suggestions:
   1. Work the entire square in latchet, punch, or rya.
   2. Work the light olive, light blue, and dark blue in latchet or punch and the balance of the square in flat stitches.

Colors and Stitches:

1	Medium Olive Flat Stem Nos. 1 and 3	8	Dark Blue Flat Stem Nos. 2 and 4
2	Medium Olive Flat Stem Nos. 2 and 4	9	Dark Olive Flat Stem Nos. 2 and 4
3	Medium Olive Continental No. 1	10	Dark Olive Flat Stem Nos. 2 and 4
4	Medium Olive Continental No. 2	11	Dark Olive Mosaic No. 1
5	Light Blue Flat Stem Nos. 1 and 3	12	Dark Olive Mosaic No. 2
6	Light Blue Flat Stem Nos. 2 and 4	13	Light Blue Continental No. 1
7	Dark Blue Flat Stem Nos. 1 and 3	14	Light Blue Continental No. 2
		15	Navy Flat Stem Nos. 1 and 3
		16	Navy Flat Stem Nos. 2 and 4
		17	Navy Continental No. 1
		18	Navy Continental No. 2

Giant Milanese
Figs. 29, 30, and Plate 10

FIG. 29

FIG. 30

Plate 10. Giant Milanese.
Other Stitch Suggestions:
* 1. Work the entire square in latchet, punch, or rya.*
* 2. Work alternate rows in latchet and rya.*

Colors and Stitches:

1 and 2	Light Purple Milanese
3 and 4	Dark Purple Milanese
5 and 6	Medium Purple Milanese
7 and 8	Dark Grayish Purple Milanese
9 and 10	Light Grayish Purple Milanese
11 and 12	Dark Bluish Purple Milanese
13 and 14	Rosish Purple Milanese
15	Medium Purple Flat Stem No. 7
16	Medium Purple Flat Stem No. 8
17	Medium Purple Flat Stem No. 5
18	Medium Purple Flat Stem No. 6
19	Rosish Purple Flat Stem No. 7
20	Rosish Purple Flat Stem No. 8
21	Rosish Purple Flat Stem No. 5
22	Rosish Purple Flat Stem No. 6

Byzantine Spires
Figs. 31, 32, 33, and Plate 11

FIG. 31

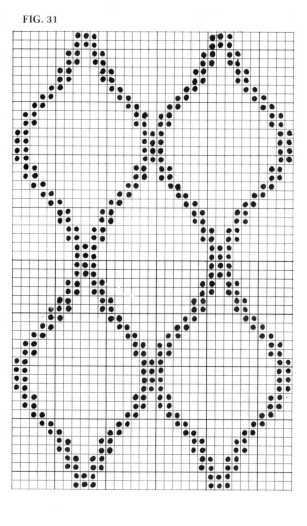

FIG. 32

FIG. 33

Plate 11. Byzantine Spires.
Other Stitch Suggestions:
    1. Work the entire square in latchet or punch.
    2. Work alternate spires in latchet and flat stitches.
    3. Work alternate rows of each spire in latchet and rya.

Colors and Stitches:

- Black Continental No. 1
Fill in with rows of colors of your
   choice.

Interlocking Bands
Figs. 34, 35, and Plate 12

FIG. 34

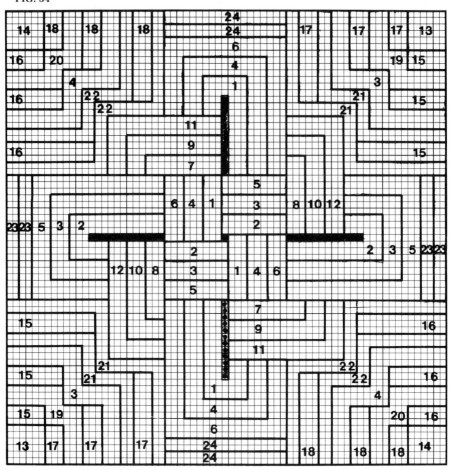

FIG. 35

Plate 12. Interlocking Banks. Executed by Ronald Wentz.
   Other Stitch Suggestions:
      1. Work the entire design in latchet, punch, or rya.
      2. Work the center motif in latchet, punch, or rya and the balance of the square in
      flat stitches.
      3. Work the center motif in rya and the balance of the square in latchet.

Colors and Stitches:

☐   Black Continental No. 1
●   Black Continental No. 2
1   Medium Blue Web No. 1
2   Medium Blue Web No. 2
3   Forest Green Scotch No. 1
4   Forest Green Scotch No. 2
5   Dark Blue Continental No. 1
6   Dark Blue Continental No. 2
7   Olive Scotch No. 1
8   Olive Scotch No. 2
9   Dark Turquoise Scotch No. 1
10   Dark Turquoise Scotch No. 2

11   Light Blue Scotch No. 1
12   Light Blue Scotch No. 2
13   Light Turquoise Scotch No. 1
14   Light Turquoise Scotch No. 2
15   Eggshell Flat Stem No. 7
16   Eggshell Flat Stem No. 8
17   Eggshell Flat Stem No. 5
18   Eggshell Flat Stem No. 6
19   Dark Blue Scotch No. 1
20   Dark Blue Scotch No. 2
21   Eggshell Flat Stem Nos. 1 and 3
22   Eggshell Flat Stem Nos. 2 and 4
23   Eggshell Flat Stem No. 1
24   Eggshell Flat Stem No. 4

Diamonds and Crosses
Figs. 36, 37, and Plate 13

FIG. 36

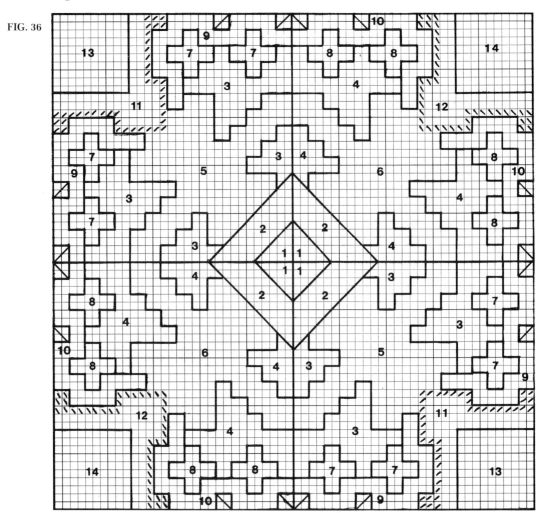

FIG 37

Plate 13. Diamonds and Crosses.
Other Stitch Suggestions:
1. Work the entire square in latchet, punch, or rya.
2. Work the gold in flat stitches and the balance of the square in latchet or punch.
3. Work the gold in latchet and the balance of the square in rya.

Colors and Stitches:

1 Navy Straight Cross
2 One row each of Dark, Medium, and Light Purple Straight Cross
3 Navy Mosaic No. 1
4 Navy Mosaic No. 2
5 Gold Continental No. 1
6 Gold Continental No. 2
7 Medium Purple Mosaic No. 1
8 Medium Purple Mosaic No. 2
9 Light Blue Mosaic No. 1
10 Light Blue Mosaic No. 2
11 Yellow Continental No. 1
12 Yellow Continental No. 2
13 Medium Blue Diagonal Mosaic No. 1
14 Medium Blue Diagonal Mosaic No. 2
/ Dark Purple Continental No. 1
\ Dark Purple Continental No. 2
⊞ Dark Purple Mosaic No. 1
⊞ Dark Purple Mosaic No. 2

Tile Number Three
Figs. 38, 39, and Plate 14

FIG. 38

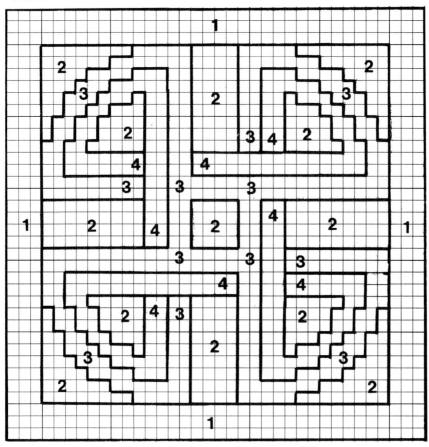

FIG. 39

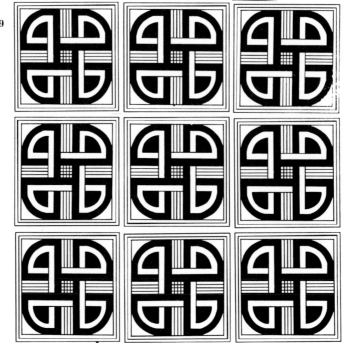

Plate 14. Tile Number Three.
Other Stitch Suggestions:
1. Work the entire square in punch or rya.
2. Work the bands in rya and the balance of the square in latchet.
3. Work the bands in latchet and the balance of the square in flat stitches (see Plate 4).

Colors and Stitches:

1 Dark Olive Web No. 1
2 Light Olive Web No. 2

3 Dark Blue Continental No. 1
4 Light Blue Continental No. 2
Stitches are reversed on alternating squares.

Aztec Motif
Figs. 40, 41, and Plate 15

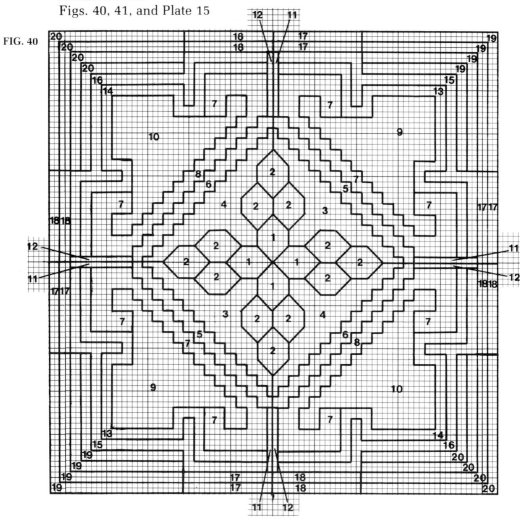

FIG. 40

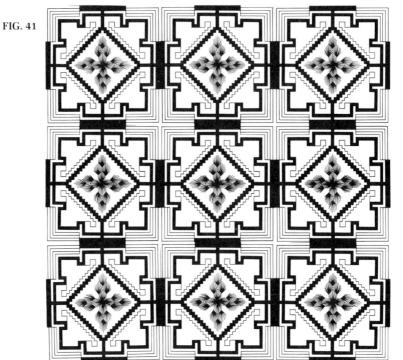

FIG. 41

40

Plate 15. Aztec Motif.
　Other Stitch Suggestions:
　　1. Work the entire square in latchet, punch, or rya.
　　2. Work the dark brown and gold in flat stitches and the balance of the square in latchet or punch.
　　3. Work the dark brown and gold in latchet and the balance of the square in rya.

Colors and Stitches:

1　Dark Blue Leaf
2　Light Blue Leaf
3　Medium Brown Continental No. 1
4　Medium Brown Continental No. 2
5 and 6　Beige Byzantine
7　Black Mosaic No. 1
8　Black Mosaic No. 1
9　Gold Continental No. 1
10　Gold Continental No. 2

11　Beige Continental No. 1
12　Beige Continental No. 2
13　Beige Mosaic No. 1
14　Beige Mosaic No. 2
15　Eggshell Mosaic No. 1
16　Eggshell Mosaic No. 2
17　Beige Flat Stem No. 1
18　Beige Flat Stem No. 2
19　Dark Brown Flat Stem Nos. 1 and 3
20　Dark Brown Flat Stem Nos. 2 and 4

41

For the Dining Room

Plate 16. Byzantine Square (see Fig. 43). The combination of Byzantine, Scotch, and Flat Stem stitches contributes to this richly textured rug design. With a design such as this, where the stitches slant in both directions, it is essential to use a frame.

Byzantine Square
Figs. 42, 43, and Plate 17

FIG. 42

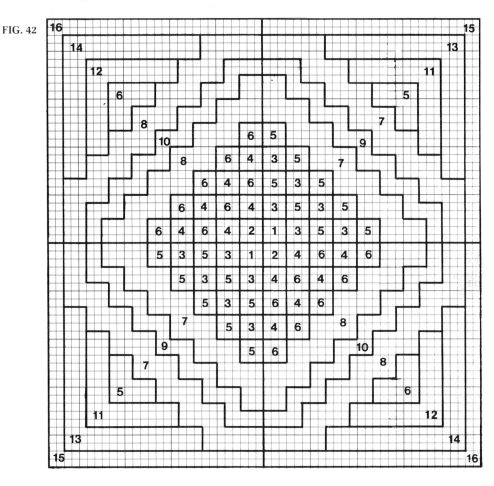

FIG. 43

44

Plate 17. Byzantine Square.
　Other Stitch Suggestions:
　　1. Work the entire square in latchet, punch, or rya.
　　2. Work the dark brown and dark orange area in rya and the balance of the square in latchet.
　　3. Work the dark brown and dark orange in latchet or punch and the balance of the design in flat stitches.
　　4. Work the area charted for Mosaic stitches in latchet and the balance of the square in flat stitches.

Colors and Stitches:

1　Orange Continental No. 1
2　Orange Continental No. 2
3　Light Brown Scotch No. 1
4　Light Brown Scotch No. 2
5　Yellow Scotch No. 1
6　Yellow Scotch No. 2
7 and 8　Dark Brown Byzantine

9 and 10　Orange Byzantine
11　Light Brown Flat Stem Nos. 5 and 7
12　Light Brown Flat Stem Nos. 6 and 8
13　Orange Flat Stem Nos. 5 and 7
14　Orange Flat Stem Nos. 6 and 8
15　Yellow Flat Stem Nos. 1 and 3
16　Yellow Flat Stem Nos. 2 and 4

Scroll Flowers
Figs. 44, 45, and Plate 18

FIG. 44

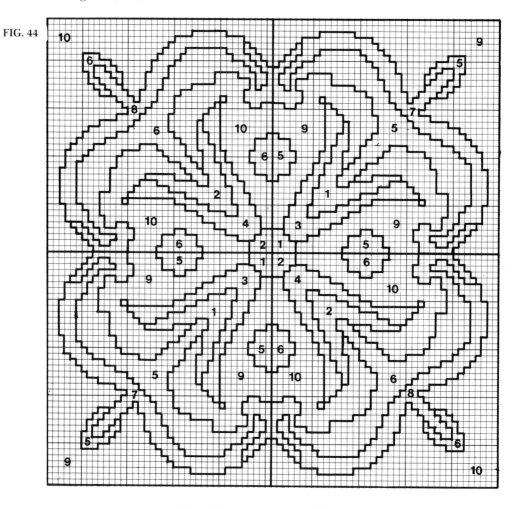

FIG. 45

Plate 18. Scroll Flowers. Executed by Sue Jane Wentz.
Other Stitch Suggestions:
1. Work the entire square in latchet, punch, or rya.
2. Work the scroll flowers in rya and the background in latchet or flat stitches.
3. Work the scroll flowers in latchet or punch and the background in flat stitches.

Colors and Stitches:

1 Light Gold Continental No. 1
2 Light Gold Continental No. 2
3 Dark Gold Continental No. 1
4 Dark Gold Continental No. 2
5 Medium Gold Continental No. 1
6 Medium Gold Continental No. 2
7 Eggshell Continental No. 1
8 Eggshell Continental No. 2
9 Dark Brown Continental No. 1
10 Dark Brown Continental No. 2

47

Leaf Stitch Center
Figs. 46, 47, and Plate 19

FIG. 46

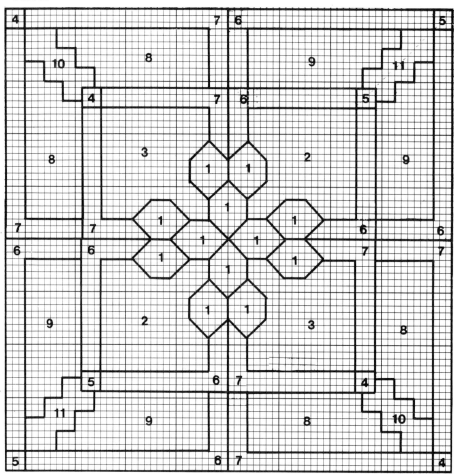

FIG. 47

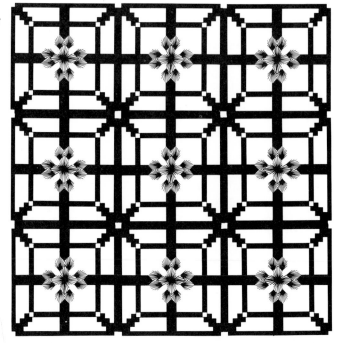

Plate 19. Leaf Stitch Center.
Other Stitch Suggestions:
1. Work the entire square in latchet, punch, or rya.
2. Work everything inside the center light blue square in rya and the balance of the square in latchet.
3. Work everything inside the center light blue square in latchet or punch and the balance of the square in flat stitches.

Colors and Stitches:

1 Dark Blue Leaf
2 Alternate Rows of Black and Brown Diagonal Mosaic No. 1
3 Alternate Rows of Black and Brown Diagonal Mosaic No. 2
4 Light Blue Scotch No. 1
5 Light Blue Scotch No. 2
6 Light Blue Flat Stem Nos. 6 and 8
7 Light Blue Flat Stem Nos. 5 and 7
8 Alternate Light and Medium Purple Scotch No. 1
9 Alternate Light and Medium Purple Scotch No. 2
10 Dark Blue Continental No. 1
11 Dark Blue Continental No. 2

Nordic Sunburst
Figs. 48, 49, and Plate 20

FIG. 48

FIG. 49

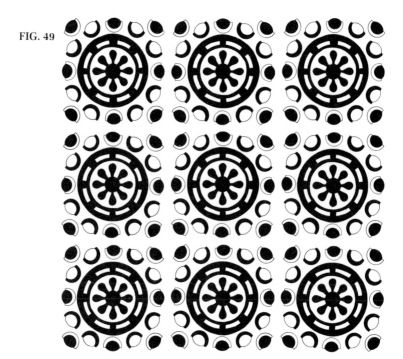

Plate 20. Nordic Sunburst.

Other Stitch Suggestions:

1. Work the entire square in latchet, punch, or rya.
2. Work the center circle in rya, the 16 half circles in latchet, and the background in flat stitches.
3. Work the center circle in punch and the balance of the square in flat stitches.
4. Work the center circle and the 16 half circles in latchet and the background in flat stitches.

Colors and Stitches:

1 Dark Plum Diagonal Mosaic No. 1
2 Dark Plum Diagonal Mosaic No. 2
3 Dark Blue Diagonal Mosaic No. 1
4 Dark Blue Diagonal Mosaic No. 2
5 Dark Blue Continental No. 1 and Flat Stem No. 5
6 Dark Blue Continental No. 2 and Flat Stem No. 6
7 Dark Blue Continental No. 1 and Flat Stem No. 7
8 Dark Blue Continental No. 2 and Flat Stem No. 8
9 Medium Blue Continental No. 1
10 Medium Blue Continental No. 2
11 Olive Diagonal Mosaic No. 1
12 Olive Diagonal Mosaic No. 2
13 Dark Green Continental No. 1
14 Dark Green Continental No. 2
15 Medium Purple Continental No. 1, Flat Stem Nos. 1 and 3
16 Medium Purple Continental No. 2, Flat Stem Nos. 2 and 4
17 Light Blue Diagonal Mosaic No. 1
18 Light Blue Diagonal Mosaic No. 2
19 Eggshell Diagonal Mosaic No. 1
20 Eggshell Diagonal Mosaic No. 2

Pennsylvania Dutch Tulips

Figs. 50, 51, and Plate 21

FIG. 50

FIG. 51

Plate 21. Pennsylvania Dutch Tulips.
   Other Stitch Suggestions:
      1. Work the entire square in latchet or punch.
      2. Work the flowers in rya and the background in latchet.
      3. Work the flowers in latchet or punch and the background in flat stitches.
      4. Work the tulips in rya, the small flowers and stems in latchet, and the background in flat stitches.

Colors and Stitches:

1 Light Yellow Continental No. 1
2 Light Yellow Continental No. 2
3 Light Gold Continental No. 1
4 Light Gold Continental No. 2
5 Dark Gold Diagonal Mosaic No. 1
6 Dark Gold Diagonal Mosaic No. 2
7 Eggshell Continental No. 1 and
     Diagonal Mosaic No. 1
8 Eggshell Continental No. 2 and
     Diagonal Mosaic No. 2
※ Green Diagonal Mosaic No. 1
※ Green Diagonal Mosaic No. 2
● Dark Gold Continental No. 1
● Dark Gold Continental No. 2
9 Dark Brown Continental No. 1
10 Dark Brown Continental No. 2

Modern Paisley
Figs. 52, 53, and Plate 22

FIG. 52

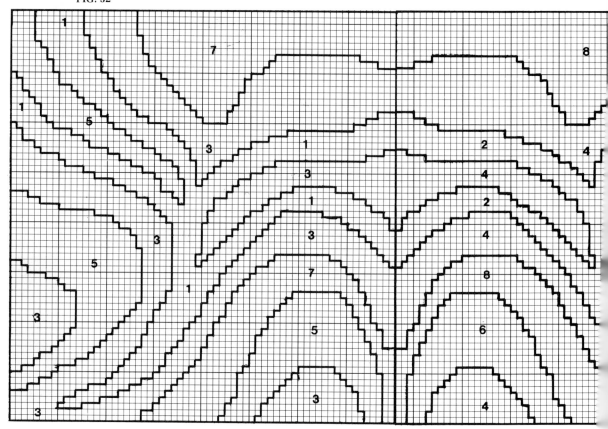

FIG. 53

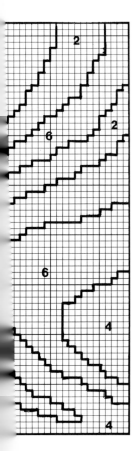

Plate 22. Modern Paisley.
   Other Stitch Suggestions:
      1. Work the entire square in latchet, punch, or rya.
      2. Work alternate rows in latchet and rya.
      3. Work alternate rows in latchet or punch and flat stitches.

Colors and Stitches:

1 Dark Blue Continental No. 1
2 Dark Blue Continental No. 2
3 Red Continental No. 1
4 Red Continental No. 2

5 Yellow Continental No. 1
6 Yellow Continental No. 2
7 Olive Continental No. 1
8 Olive Continental No. 2

Indian Motif Number One

Figs. 54, 55, and Plate 23

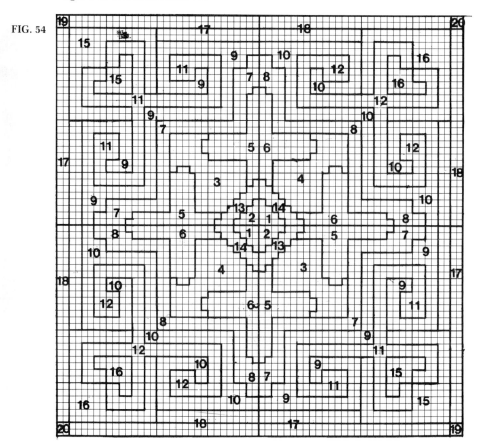

FIG. 54

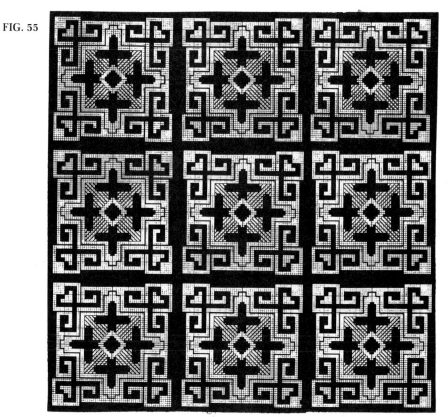

FIG. 55

56

Plate 23. Indian Motif Number One.
  Other Stitch Suggestions:
    1. Work the entire square in latchet, punch, or rya.
    2. Work the gold, light yellow, medium brown, and dark blue in rya and the balance
    of the design in latchet.
    3. Work the gold, light yellow, medium brown, and dark blue in latchet or punch and
    the balance of the design in flat stitches.

Colors and Stitches:

1 and 2   Single Gold Milanese
3   Medium Blue Diagonal Mosaic
      No. 1
4   Medium Blue Diagonal Mosaic
      No. 2
5   Medium Brown Continental No. 1
6   Medium Brown Continental No. 2
7   Gold Mosaic No. 1
8   Gold Mosaic No. 2
9   Light Blue Mosaic No. 1
10   Light Blue Mosaic No. 2
11   Dark Blue Mosaic No. 1
12   Dark Blue Mosaic No. 2
13   Light Yellow Continental No. 1
14   Light Yellow Continental No. 2
15   Medium Yellow Mosaic No. 1
16   Medium Yellow Mosaic No. 2
17   Dark Brown Flat Stem Nos. 1 and 3
18   Dark Brown Flat Stem Nos. 2 and 4
19   Dark Brown Mosaic No. 1
20   Dark Brown Mosaic No. 2

Modern Sunburst
Figs. 56, 57, and Plate 24

FIG. 56

FIG. 57

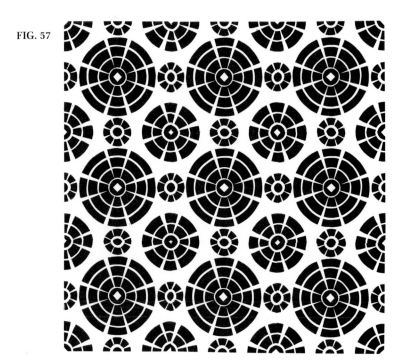

Plate 24. Modern Sunburst.

  Other Stitch Suggestions:
    1. Work the entire square in latchet, punch, or rya.
    2. Work the large center circle in rya, the smaller circles in latchet, and the background in flat stitches.
    3. Work all the circles in latchet or punch and the background in flat stitches.
    4. Work the large center circle in latchet or punch and the balance of the square in flat stitches.

Colors and Stitches:

1 and 2   Single Dark Brown Milanese
3   Light Orange Diagonal Mosaic No. 1
4   Light Orange Diagonal Mosaic No. 2
5   Medium Orange Diagonal Mosaic No. 1
6   Medium Orange Diagonal Mosaic No. 2
7   Dark Orange Diagonal Mosaic No. 1
8   Dark Orange Diagonal Mosaic No. 2
9   Rust Diagonal Mosaic No. 1
10   Rust Diagonal Mosaic No. 2
11   Dark Brown Continental No. 1
12   Dark Brown Continental No. 2
13   Yellow Diagonal Mosaic No. 1
14   Yellow Diagonal Mosaic No. 2
15   Dark Green Continental No. 1
16   Dark Green Continental No. 2

Indian Motif Number Two

Figs. 58, 59, and Plate 25

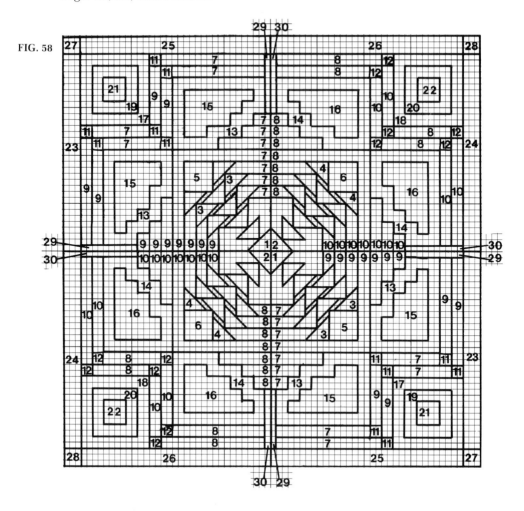

FIG. 58

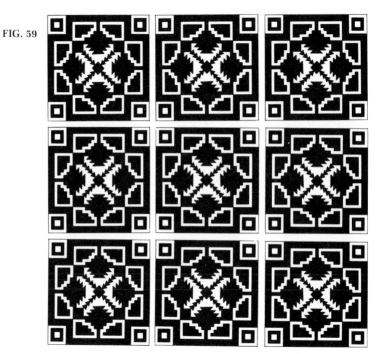

FIG. 59

60

Plate 25. Indian Motif Number Two.
  Other Stitch Suggestions:
    1. Work the entire square in latchet, punch, or rya.
    2. Work the turquoise, medium brown, dark brown, and light blue in latchet and the balance of the design in rya.
    3. Work the turquoise, medium brown, dark brown, and light blue in flat stitches and the balance of the design in latchet or punch.

Colors and Stitches:

1 and 2	Dark Olive Milanese	17	Black Mosaic No. 1
3 and 4	Navy Milanese	18	Black Mosaic No. 2
5	Dark Brown Continental No. 1	19	Light Olive Mosaic No. 1
6	Dark Brown Continental No. 2	20	Light Olive Mosaic No. 2
7	Turquoise Flat Stem No. 3	21	Navy Mosaic No. 1
8	Turquoise Flat Stem No. 4	22	Navy Mosaic No. 2
9	Turquoise Flat Stem No. 1	23	Medium Brown Flat Stem No. 5
10	Turquoise Flat Stem No. 2	24	Medium Brown Flat Stem No. 6
11 and 12	Turquoise Milanese	25	Medium Brown Flat Stem No. 7
13	Dark Brown Mosaic No. 1	26	Medium Brown Flat Stem No. 8
14	Dark Brown Mosaic No. 2	27	Medium Brown Scotch No. 1
15	Light Blue Mosaic No. 1	28	Medium Brown Scotch No. 2
16	Light Blue Mosaic No. 2	29	Turquoise Continental No. 1
		30	Turquoise Continental No. 2

For the Bedroom

Plate 26. Tree of Life Quilt Design (see Fig. 73). This classic American quilt design has been made into a hall runner with a technique popular in early American rugs—the punch stitch. This richly textured stitch is as delightful to the eye as it is to the foot.

Giant Persian

Figs. 60, 61, and Plate 27

FIG. 60

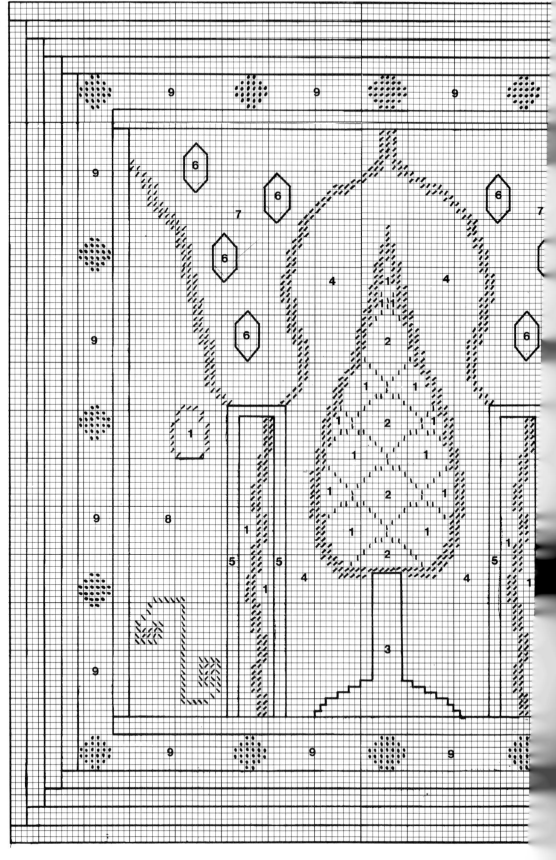

FIG. 61

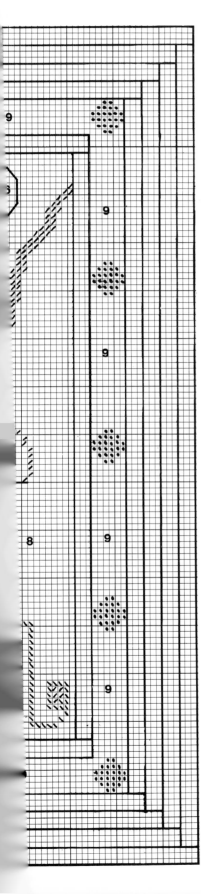

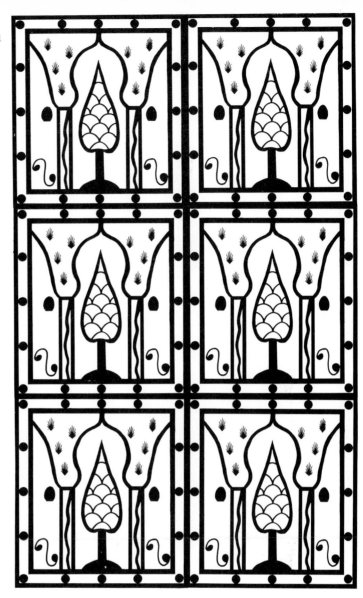

Colors and Stitches:

1   Medium Orange Continental No. 1
2   Rust Continental No. 1
3   Black Continental No. 1
4   Brown Mosaic No. 1
5   Medium Gold Mosaic No. 2
6   Medium Gold Leaf
7   Medium Orange Mosaic No. 1
8   White Continental No. 1
9   White Mosaic No. 1
Unnumbered Borders—Black Flat Stem
   Nos. 5, 6, 7, and 8
  /   Black Continental No. 1
  | Dark Gold Continental No. 1
  •   Medium Orange Continental No. 1
  \   Medium Gold Continental No. 1

Plate 27. Giant Persian Design.
   Other Stitch Suggestions:
      1. Work the entire design in latchet, punch, or rya.
      2. Work the inside black border and everything inside in rya and the balance of the square in latchet.
      3. Work the black and eggshell portions of the square in flat stitches and the balance of the square in latchet or punch.

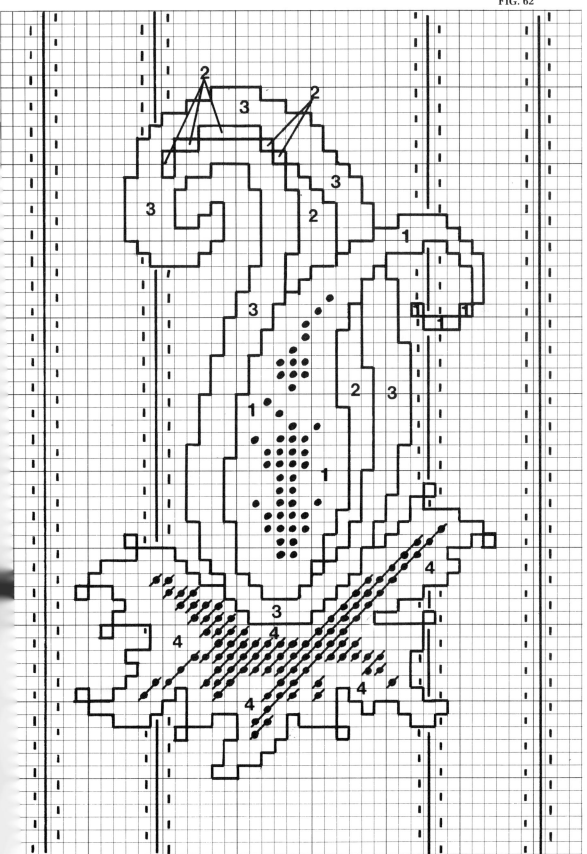

FIG. 63

Plate 28. Small Paisley
  Other Stitch Suggestions:
    1. Work the entire rectangle in latchet, punch, or rya.
    2. Work the paisley in rya and the stripes and background in latchet.
    3. Work the paisley in latchet or punch and the stripes and background in flat stitches.

Colors and Stitches:

1 Medium Blue Continental No. 1
2 Dark Purple Continental No. 1
3 Medium Purple Continental No. 1

4 Light Lavender Continental No. 1
● Dark Blue Continental No. 1
| Dark Purple Continental No. 1
⚲ Medium Lavender Continental No. 1
Background—Black Continental No. 1

Paisley with Border
Figs. 64, 65, and Plate 29

FIG. 64

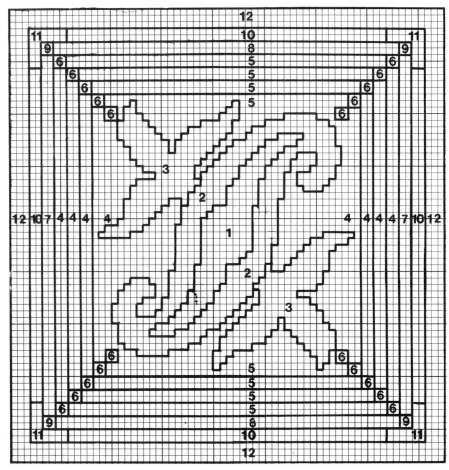

FIG. 65

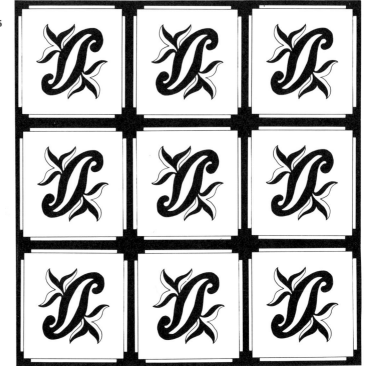

Plate 29. Paisley with Border.
Other Stitch Suggestions:
    1. Work the entire design in latchet, punch, or rya.
    2. Work the gold, blue, red, and black in rya and the balance of the square in latchet.
    3. Work the gold, blue, red, and black in latchet, punch, or rya and the balance of the square in flat stitches.

Colors and Stitches:

1	Gold Diagonal Mosaic No. 1	6	Medium Lavender Mosaic No. 1
2	Blue Diagonal Mosaic No. 1	7	Dark Lavender Flat Stem No. 2
3	Dark Red Continental No. 1	8	Dark Lavender Flat Stem No. 4
4	Medium Lavender Flat Stem No. 1	9	Dark Lavender Mosaic No. 2
5	Medium Lavender Flat Stem No. 3	10	Eggshell Mosaic No. 2
		11	Black Mosaic No. 2
		12	Black Scotch No. 2

Giant Flower

Figs. 66, 67, and Plate 30

FIG. 66

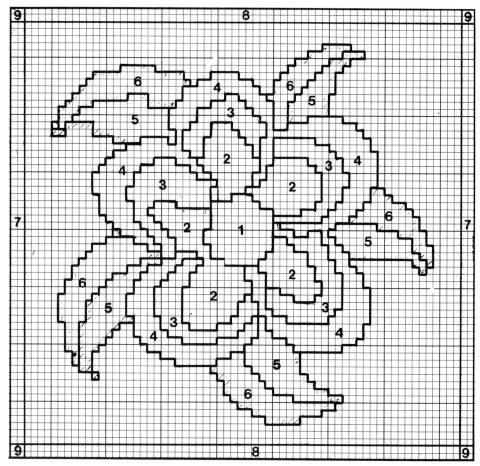

FIG. 67

72

Plate 30. Giant Flower.
   Other Stitch Suggestions:
      1. Work the entire square in latchet or rya.
      2. Work the flower and leaves in rya, the outside border in latchet, and the background in flat stitches.
      3. Work the flower, leaves, and border in latchet or punch and the background in flat stitches.

Colors and Flat Stitches:

1 Rust Punch
2 Dark Orange Diagonal Mosaic No. 1
3 Medium Orange Diagonal Mosaic
      No. 1
4 Light Orange Continental No. 1
5 Light Olive Diagonal Mosaic No. 1
6 Dark Olive Diagonal Mosaic No. 1
7 Dark Olive Flat Stem No. 1
8 Dark Olive Flat Stem No. 3
9 Dark Olive Mosaic No. 1
Background—Medium Brown Mosaic
      No. 1

Punch Colors:

1 Brown
2 Gold
3 Light Orange
4 Medium Orange
5 Light Green
6 Dark Green
Background—Eggshell

73

Stepping Stones Quilt Design
Figs. 68, 69, and Plate 31

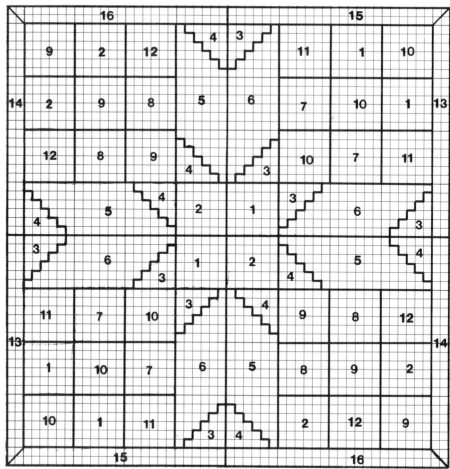

FIG. 68

FIG. 69

74

Plate 31. Stepping Stones Quilt Design.
Other Stitch Suggestions:
1. Work the entire square in latchet, punch, or rya.
2. Work the light blue, pink, and medium blue in rya and the balance of the square in latchet.
3. Work the light blue, pink, medium blue, and dark blue border in latchet or punch and the balance of the design in flat stitches.
4. Work the light blue square in the center in rya, the medium blue and pink in latchet, and the balance of the square in flat stitches.

Colors and Stitches:

1	Light Blue Mosaic No. 1	8	Dark Blue Continental No. 2
2	Light Blue Mosaic No. 2	9	Maroon Web No. 1
3	Pink Continental No. 1	10	Maroon Web No. 2
4	Pink Continental No. 2	11	Dark Red Mosaic No. 1
5	Medium Blue Web No. 1	12	Dark Red Mosaic No. 2
6	Medium Blue Web No. 2	13	Dark Blue Flat Stem No. 1
7	Dark Blue Continental No. 1	14	Dark Blue Flat Stem No. 2
		15	Dark Blue Flat Stem No. 3
		16	Dark Blue Flat Stem No. 4

Pennsylvania Dutch Roses

Figs. 70, 71, and Plate 32

FIG. 70

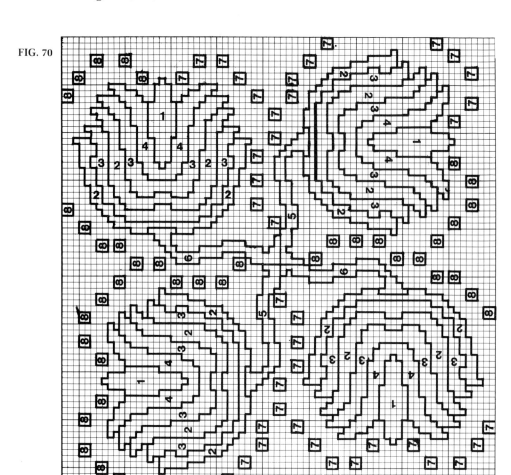

FIG. 71

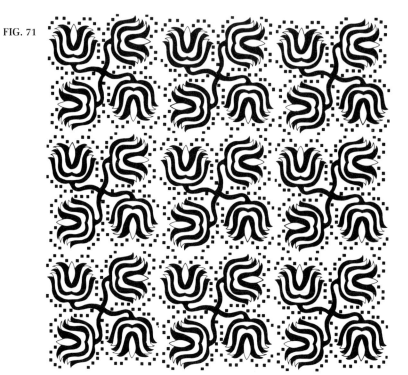

76

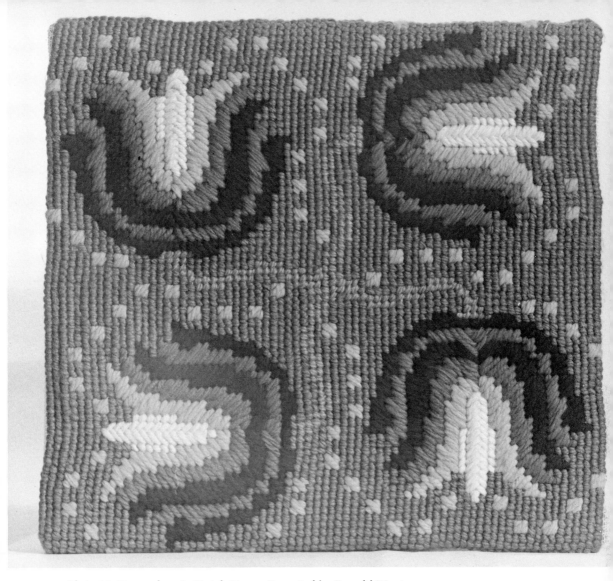

Plate 32. Pennsylvania Dutch Roses. Executed by Ronald Wentz.
   Other Stitch Suggestions:
      1. Work the entire square in latchet, punch, or rya.
      2. Work the roses and stems in rya and the balance of the square in latchet.
      3. Work the roses in latchet or punch and the balance of the square in flat stitches.

Colors and Stitches:

The Diagonal Satin Stitches slant from the outside of the flower upward toward the center of the flower.

1 Light Pink Fern with a single row of Light Pink Continental No. 1 on the left side and a single row of Light Pink Continental No. 2 on the right side

2 Dark Rose Diagonal Satin
3 Medium Rose Diagonal Satin
4 Light Rose Diagonal Satin
5 Olive Continental No. 1
6 Olive Continental No. 2
7 Light Rose Mosaic No. 1
Background—Light Blue Continental No. 1

77

Tree of Life Quilt Design
Figs. 72, 73, and Plate 33

FIG. 72

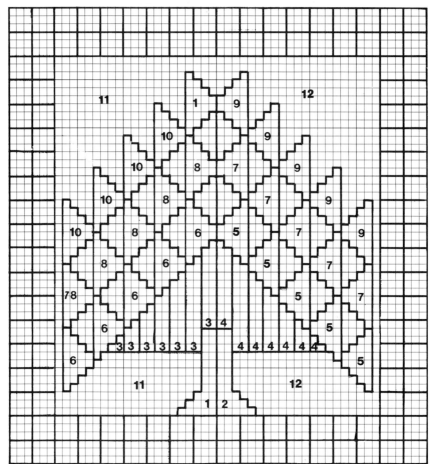

FIG. 73

Plate 33. Tree of Life Quilt Design.
Other Stitch Suggestions:

1. Work the entire square in latchet or rya.

2. Work the tree in rya and the balance of the square in latchet.

3. Work the tree in latchet or punch and the balance of the square in flat stitches.

Colors and Flat Stitches:

1 Dark Brown Continental No. 2
2 Dark Brown Continental No. 1
3 Dark Olive Flat Stem No. 2
4 Dark Olive Flat Stem No. 1
5 Dark Maroon Web No. 1
6 Dark Maroon Web No. 2
7 Dark Red Web No. 1
8 Dark Red Web No. 2
9 Red Web No. 1
10 Red Web No. 2
11 Eggshell Scotch No. 1
12 Eggshell Scotch No. 2
Unmarked Triangles in Left Side of Tree—Eggshell Continental No. 1
Unmarked Triangles in Right Side of Tree—Eggshell Continental No. 2

Outside Border, Right Half—Alternate Dark Olive and Eggshell Scotch No. 2
Outside Border, Left Half—Alternate Dark Olive and Eggshell Scotch No. 1

Punch Colors:

1 and 2 Dark Brown
3 and 4 Dark Green
5 through 10 Light Blue
Unmarked Triangles inside Tree—Gold
11 and 12 Eggshell
Outside Border—Dark Blue

Flying Geese Quilt Design
Figs. 74, 75, and Plate 34

FIG. 74

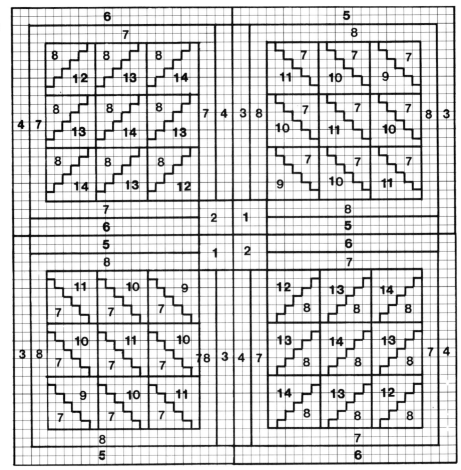

FIG. 75

Plate 34. Flying Geese Quilt Design.
  Other Stitch Suggestions:
    1. Work the entire square in latchet, punch, or rya.
    2. Work the black square in the center and the red and black triangles in rya and the balance of the square in latchet.
    3. Work the black square in the center, the red and black triangles, and the outside border in latchet or punch and the balance of the square in flat stitches.

Colors and Stitches:

  1 Black Continental No. 1
  2 Black Continental No. 2
  3 Gray Flat Stem No. 1
  4 Gray Flat Stem No. 2
  5 Gray Flat Stem No. 3

  6 Gray Flat Stem No. 4
  7 Eggshell Web No. 2
  8 Eggshell Web No. 1
  9 and 12   Red Diagonal Satin
  10 and 13   Maroon Diagonal Satin
  11 and 14   Black Diagonal Satin

Stained Glass
Figs. 76, 77, and Plate 35

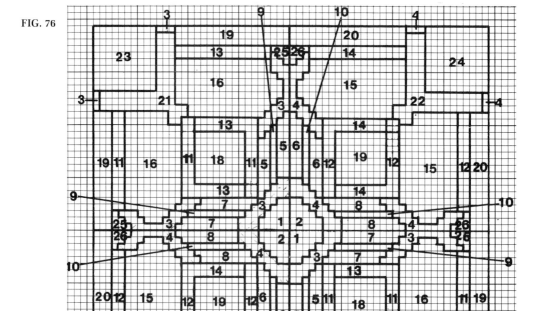

FIG. 76

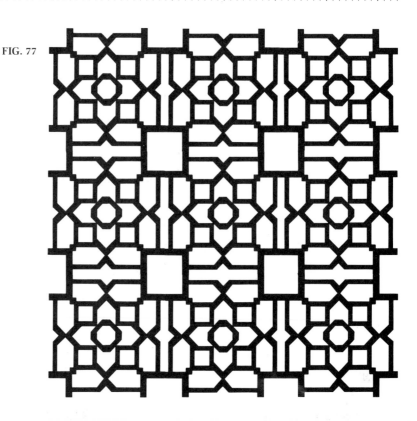

FIG. 77

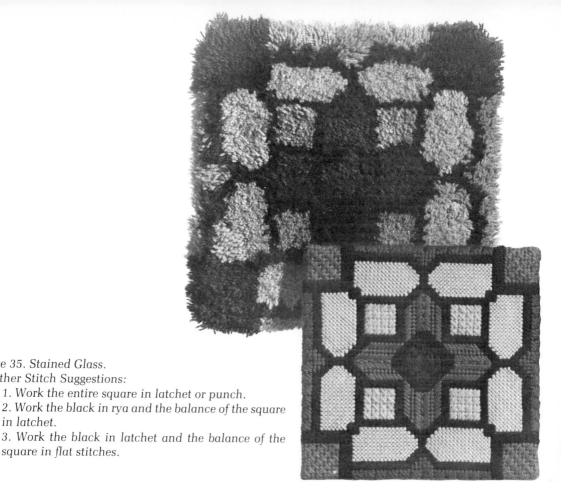

Plate 35. Stained Glass.
  Other Stitch Suggestions:
    1. Work the entire square in latchet or punch.
    2. Work the black in rya and the balance of the square in latchet.
    3. Work the black in latchet and the balance of the square in flat stitches.

Colors and Flat Stitches:

1	Maroon Diagonal Mosaic No. 1
2	Maroon Diagonal Mosaic No. 2
3	Black Continental No. 1
4	Black Continental No. 2
5	Dark Blue Flat Stem No. 1
6	Dark Blue Flat Stem No. 2
7	Dark Blue Flat Stem No. 3
8	Dark Blue Flat Stem No. 4
9	Dark Blue Continental No. 1
10	Dark Blue Continental No. 2
11	Black Flat Stem No. 1
12	Black Flat Stem No. 2
13	Black Flat Stem No. 3
14	Black Flat Stem No. 4
15	Light Blue Web No. 1
16	Light Blue Web No. 2
17	Pink Mosaic No. 1
18	Pink Mosaic No. 2
19	Maroon Scotch No. 1
20	Maroon Scotch No. 2
21	Black Scotch No. 1
22	Black Scotch No. 2
23	Dark Lavender Diagonal Mosaic No. 1
24	Dark Lavender Diagonal Mosaic No. 2
25	Maroon Continental No. 1
26	Maroon Continental No. 2

Rya Colors:

1, 2, 5, 6, 7, 8, 9, 10, 23, and 24   Dark Blue
15 and 16   Light Blue
17, 18, 19, and 20   Olive
3, 4, 11, 12, 13, 14, 21, and 22   Charcoal Gray

83

For the
Den or Library

Plate 36. Aztec Priest (see Fig. 83). Our friendly Aztec Priest has been outlined with a portion of the Indian Motif Number Three to create a handsome wall hanging. The design would be equally effective as a hall runner.

Indian Motif Number Three
Figs. 78, 79, and Plate 37

FIG. 78

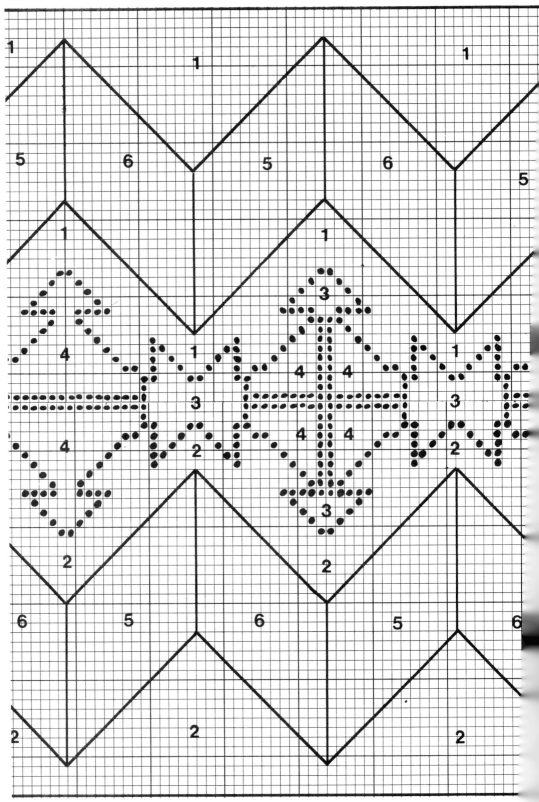

FIG. 79

Colors and Stitches:

1   Medium Brown Continental No. 1
2   Medium Brown Continental No. 2
3   Yellow Continental No. 1
4   Gold Continental No. 1
5   Alternate rows of Medium Brown, Light Gold, Rust, Dark Gold   Diagonal Gobelin No. 1
6   Alternate rows of Medium Brown, Light Gold, Rust, Dark Gold   Diagonal Gobelin No. 2
●   Yellow Continental No. 1

87

Plate 37. Indian Motif Number Three.
   Other Stitch Suggestions:
      1. Work the entire square in latchet, punch, or rya.
      2. Work the zigzag bands and center motif in latchet, punch, or rya and the background in flat stitches.
      3. Work the center motif in rya, the zigzag bands in latchet, and the background in flat stitches.

Indian Eagle
Figs. 80, 81, and Plate 38

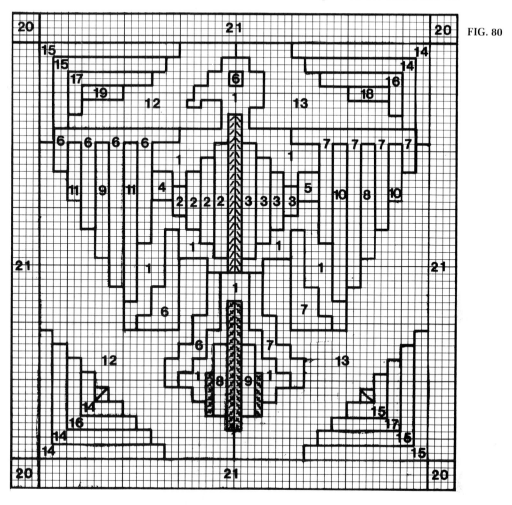

FIG. 80

FIG. 81

Plate 38. Indian Eagle.
Other Stitch Suggestions:
1. Work the entire square in latchet, punch, or rya.
2. Work the eagle in latchet or punch and the balance of the square in flat stitches.
3. Work the eagle in rya, the eggshell circle in latchet, and the balance of the square in flat stitches.

Colors and Stitches:

/	Gold Continental No. 1
\	Gold Continental No. 2
+	Dark Orange Continental No. 1
×	Dark Orange Continental No. 2
⊞	Rust Mosaic No. 1
⊞	Rust Mosaic No. 2
1	Olive Continental No. 1
2	Gold Flat Stem No. 1
3	Gold Flat Stem No. 2
4	Gold Continental No. 1
5	Gold Continental No. 2
6	Yellow Mosaic No. 1
7	Yellow Mosaic No. 2
8	Dark Orange Mosaic No. 1
9	Dark Orange Mosaic No. 2
10	Light Orange Mosaic No. 1
11	Light Orange Mosaic No. 2
12	Eggshell Continental No. 1
13	Eggshell Continental No. 2
14	Green Flat Stem Nos. 1 and 3
15	Green Flat Stem Nos. 2 and 4
16	Rust Flat Stem Nos. 1 and 3
17	Rust Flat Stem Nos. 2 and 4
18	Green Flat Stem No. 3
19	Green Flat Stem No. 4
20	Black Continental No. 1
21	Two rows of Flat Stem Nos. 1 and 3 in irregular blocks of Black and Olive

COLOR PLATE 1

See keyed diagrams on pages 214 and 215 for explanation of each item in these color plates.

COLOR PLATE 6

COLOR PLATE 7 >

COLOR PLATE 8

FIG. 82

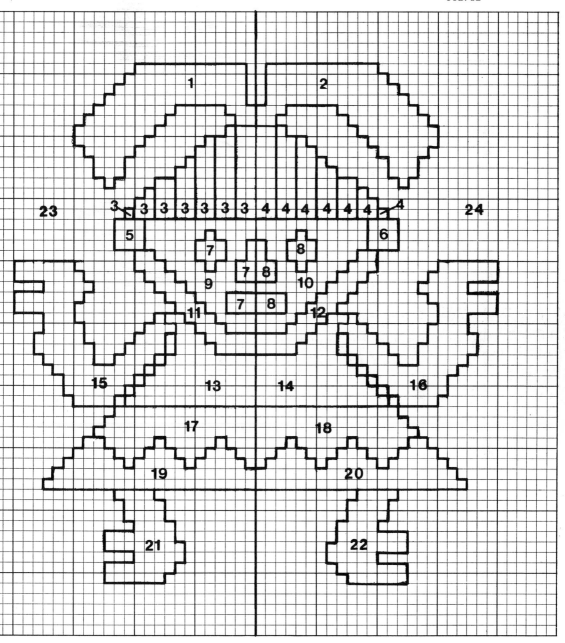

FIG. 83

Plate 39. Aztec Priest.

Other Stitch Suggestions:

1. Work the entire design in rya or punch (see Plate 36).
2. Work the priest in rya and the background in latchet or flat stitches.
3. Work the priest in punch and the background in flat . stitches.

Colors and Flat Stitches:

1 Medium Orange Diagonal Mosaic No. 1
2 Medium Orange Diagonal Mosaic No. 2
3 Rust Flat Stem No. 1
4 Rust Flat Stem No. 2
5 Medium Brown Scotch No. 1
6 Medium Brown Scotch No. 2
7 Dark Brown Continental No. 1
8 Dark Brown Continental No. 2
9 Tan Continental No. 1
10 Tan Continental No. 2
11 Dark Brown Diagonal Mosaic No. 1
12 Dark Brown Diagonal Mosaic No. 2
13 Gold Diagonal Mosaic No. 1
14 Gold Diagonal Mosaic No. 2
15 Gold Continental No. 1
16 Gold Continental No. 2
17 Bright Orange Diagonal Mosaic No. 1
18 Bright Orange Diagonal Mosaic No. 2
19 Yellow Diagonal Mosaic No. 1
20 Yellow Diagonal Mosaic No. 2
21 Olive Continental No. 1
22 Olive Continental No. 2
23 Eggshell Diagonal Mosaic No. 1
24 Eggshell Diagonal Mosaic No. 2

Latchet Colors:

1 and 2   Light Orange
3, 4, 21, and 22   Rust
5, 6, 11, and 12   Medium Brown
7 and 8   Black
9 and 10   Light Gold
13, 14, 15, and 16   Medium Orange
17 and 18   Medium Gold
19 and 20   Dark Gold
23   Eggshell Mosaic No. 1
24   Eggshell Mosaic No. 2
Border—Light, Medium, and Dark Gold Latchet

Indian Motif Number Four
Figs. 84, 85, 86, and Plate 40

FIG. 84

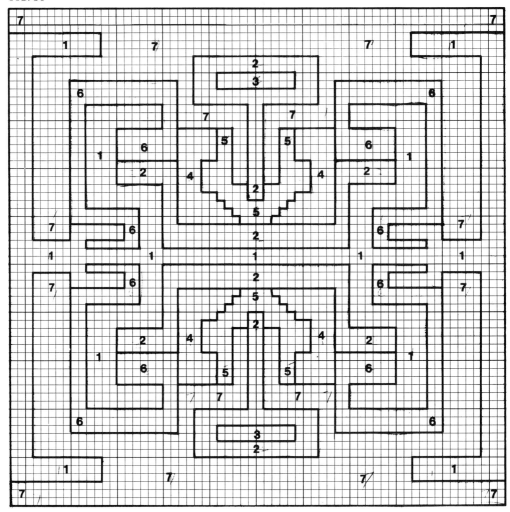

FIG. 85

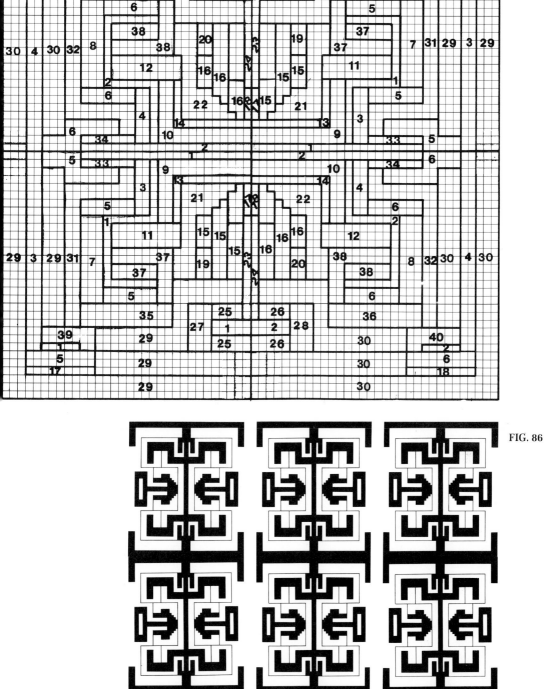

FIG. 86

Plate 40. Indian Motif Number Four. Executed by Ronald Wentz.
  Other Stitch Suggestions:
  1. Work the entire square in latchet or rya.
  2. Work alternate color areas in latchet and rya.
  3. Work alternate color areas in punch and flat stitches.

Colors and Flat Stitches:

1   Orange Continental No. 1
2   Orange Continental No. 2
3   Orange Flat Stem No. 1
4   Orange Flat Stem No. 2
5   Orange Flat Stem No. 3
6   Orange Flat Stem No. 4
7   Orange Flat Stem No. 5
8   Orange Flat Stem No. 6
9   White Mosaic No. 1
10   White Mosaic No. 2
11   White Scotch No. 1
12   White Scotch No. 2
13   White Continental No. 1
14   White Continental No. 2
15   Black Flat Stem No. 1
16   Black Flat Stem No. 2
17   Black Continental No. 1
18   Black Continental No. 2
19   Light Gold Flat Stem No. 1
20   Light Gold Flat Stem No. 2
21   Light Gold Flat Stem Nos. 1, 3, and 5
22   Light Gold Flat Stem Nos. 2, 4, and 6
23   Dark Gold Continental No. 1
24   Dark Gold Continental No. 2

25   Dark Gold Mosaic No. 1
26   Dark Gold Mosaic No. 2
27   Dark Gold Scotch No. 1
28   Dark Gold Scotch No. 2
29   Medium Gold Scotch No. 1
30   Medium Gold Scotch No. 2
31   Olive Mosaic No. 1
32   Olive Mosaic No. 2
32   Olive Continental No. 1
34   Olive Continental No. 2
35   Olive Scotch No. 1
36   Olive Scotch No. 2
37   Olive Flat Stem Nos. 1 and 3
38   Olive Flat Stem Nos. 2 and 4
39   Medium Gold Flat Stem No. 3
40   Medium Gold Flat Stem No. 4

Punch Colors:

1   Gold
2   Light Orange
3   Dark Orange
4   Eggshell
5   Light Brown
6   Red
7   Dark Brown

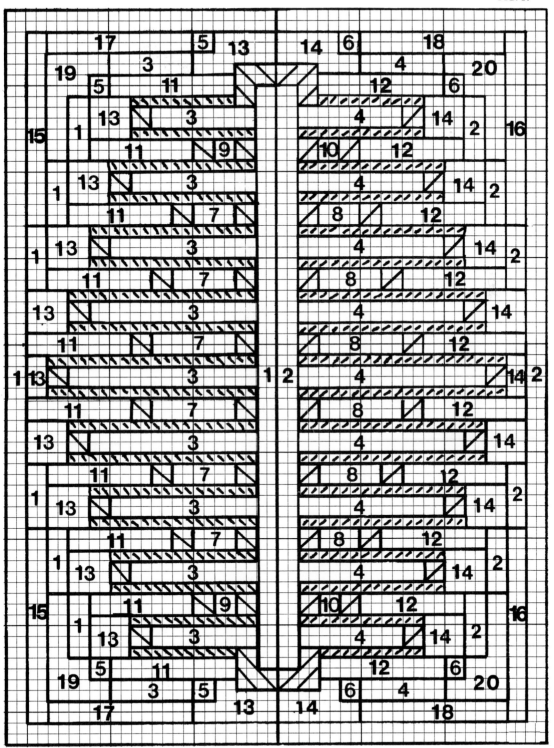

FIG. 88

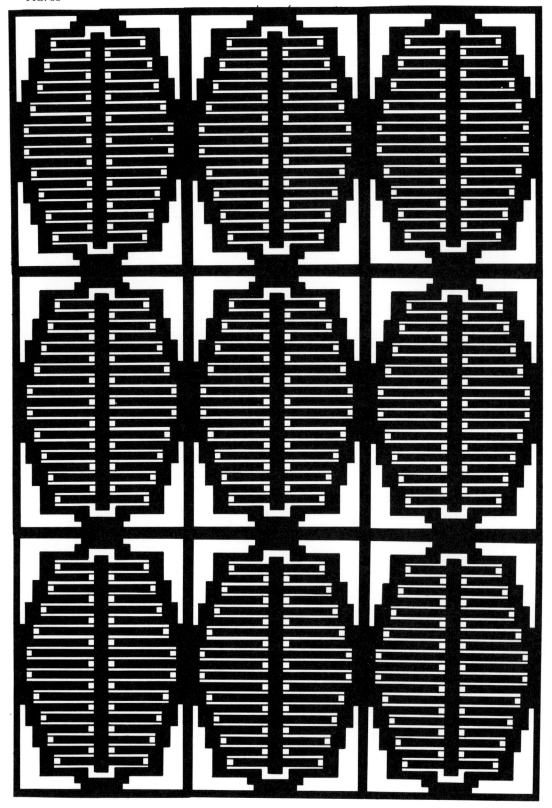

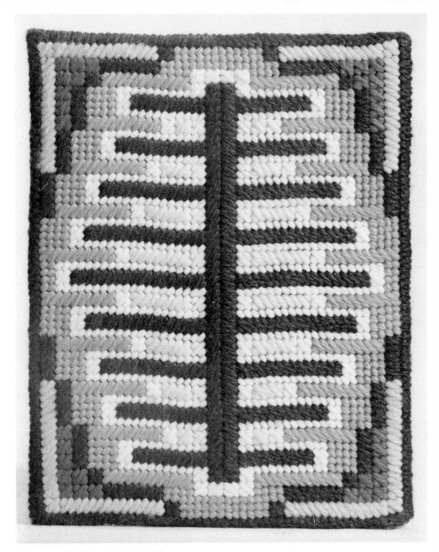

Plate 41. Indian Tree Motif.
Other Stitch Suggestions:
 1. Work the entire rectangle in latchet, punch, or rya.
 2. Work the tree motif in rya and the balance of the rectangle in latchet or flat stitches.
 3. Work the tree motif in latchet or punch and the balance of the rectangle in flat stitches.

Colors and Stitches:

1	Dark Olive Flat Stem No. 1	12	Dark Orange Flat Stem No. 4
2	Dark Olive Flat Stem No. 2	13	Dark Orange Continental No. 1
3	Dark Olive Flat Stem No. 3	14	Dark Orange Continental No. 2
4	Dark Olive Flat Stem No. 4	15	Light Orange Flat Stem No. 1
5	Dark Olive Mosaic No. 1	16	Light Orange Flat Stem No. 2
6	Dark Olive Mosaic No. 2	17	Light Orange Flat Stem No. 3
7	Yellow Flat Stem No. 3	18	Light Orange Flat Stem No. 4
8	Yellow Flat Stem No. 4	19	Brown Mosaic No. 1
9	Yellow Mosaic No. 1	20	Brown Mosaic No. 2
10	Yellow Mosaic No. 2	/	Eggshell Continental No. 1
11	Dark Orange Flat Stem No. 3	\	Eggshell Continental No. 2
		⊞	Eggshell Mosaic No. 1
		⊞	Eggshell Mosaic No. 2

Lion Rampant
Figs. 89, 90, and Plate 42

FIG. 89

FIG. 90

Colors and Stitches:

●   Light Gold Continental No. 1
/   Red Continental No. 1
×   Black Continental No. 1
| Dark Gold Continental No. 1

The balance of the design is worked in
  Light Gold Continental No. 1
Background—Dark Green Continental
  No. 1

Plate 42. Lion Rampant.

Other Stitch Suggestions:

1. Work the entire square in latchet, punch, or rya.

2. Work the lion in latchet, punch, or rya and the balance of the square in flat stitches.

3. Work the lion in rya and the balance of the square in latchet.

FIG. 92

Plate 43. Heraldic Eagle.
Other Stitch Suggestions:
    1. Work the entire square in latchet, punch, or rya.
    2. Work the eagle in rya and the background in latchet.
    3. Work the eagle in latchet or punch and the background in flat stitches.

Colors and Stitches:

• Dark Gold Continental No. 1
/ Olive Continental No. 2

1 Light Gold Continental No. 1
2 Tan Continental No. 1
Background—Olive Mosaic No. 1

Shields

Figs. 93, 94, and Plate 44

FIG. 93

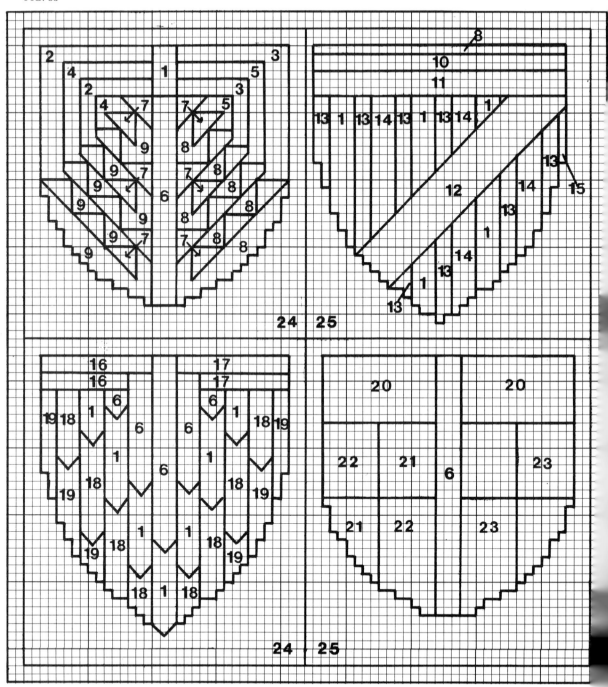

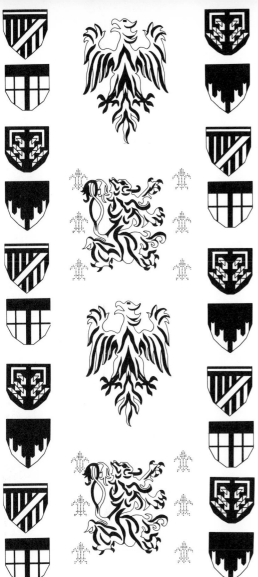

FIG. 94

12 Dark Blue Diagonal Mosaic No. 1
13 Gold Flat Stem No. 2
14 Dark Olive Fern
15 Gold Continental No. 1
16 Dark Blue Flat Stem No. 4
17 Dark Blue Flat Stem No. 3
18 Maroon Fern
19 Pink Fern (only half of the stitch is
      used on the outside edges)
20 Alternate Yellow and Brown
      Mosaic No. 1
21 Lavender Continental No. 1
22 Light Blue Web No. 1
23 Pink Knotted
24 Eggshell Mosaic No. 1
25 Eggshell Mosaic No. 2
Border—Red Flat Stem Nos. 1, 2, 3,
  and 4

Rya Colors:

UPPER LEFT SHIELD

1, 2, and 4   Rust
4 and 6   Olive
7   Dark Blue
8 and 9   Dark Gold

UPPER RIGHT SHIELD

8, 10, and 12   Dark Blue
11   Olive
1, 14, and 15   Rust
13   Dark Gold

LOWER LEFT SHIELD

6, 16, and 17   Dark Plum
1   Light Blue
18   Light Gold
19   Dark Blue

LOWER RIGHT SHIELD

20   Alternate Red and Rust
22   Light Gold
21   Dark Blue
8   Dark Gold
23   Plum
Background—White

Colors and Flat Stitches:

1 Dark Purple Fern
2 Dark Purple Flat Stem Nos. 2
    and 4
3 Dark Purple Flat Stem Nos. 1
    and 3
4 Dark Brown Flat Stem Nos. 2
    and 4
5 Dark Brown Flat Stem Nos. 1
    and 3
6 Dark Blue Fern
7 Pink Milanese
8 Maroon Continental No. 1
9 Maroon Continental No. 2
10 Maroon Flat Stem No. 3
11 Red Web No. 1

Plate 44. Shields.
  Other Stitch Suggestions:
    1. Work the entire square in latchet or punch.
    2. Work the shields in rya and the background in latchet.
    3. Work the shields in latchet or punch and the background in flat stitches.

FIG. 95

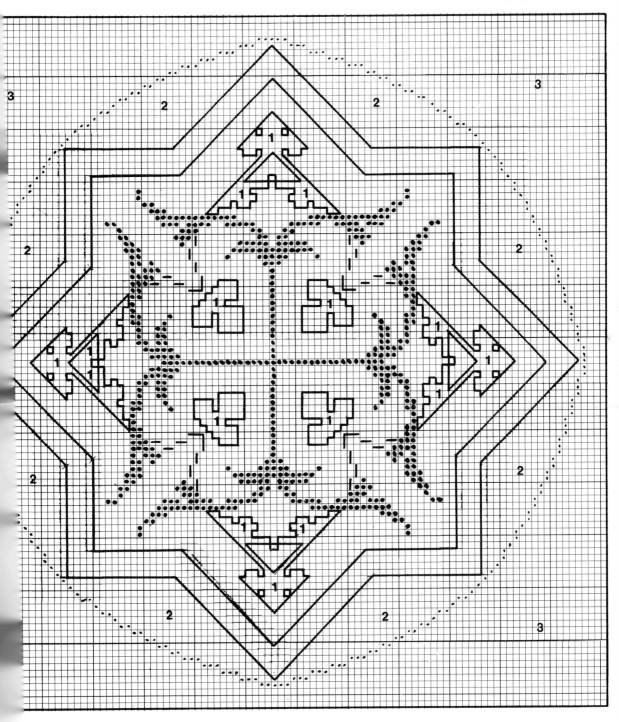

FIG. 96

Plate 45. Florentine Tile.
  Other Stitch Suggestions:
    1. Work the entire square in latchet or punch.
    2. Work the star and everything inside it in latchet or punch and the balance of the
  square in flat stitches.

Colors and Stitches:

● Dark Blue Continental No. 1
╪ Medium Blue Continental No. 1
● Dark Blue Continental No. 1
1 Medium Blue Continental No. 1

2 Light Blue Continental No. 1
3 Dark Blue Continental No. 1
Background Inside Star—Light Blue
  Continental No. 1
Star—Medium Blue Continental No. 1

Key on Broken Cane
Figs. 97, 98, and Plate 46

FIG. 97

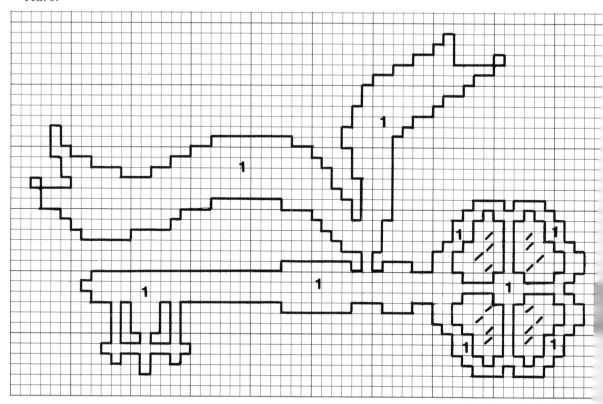

FIG. 98

Plate 46. Key on Broken Cane.
   Other Stitch Suggestions:
      1. Work the entire square in latchet or punch.
      2. Work the key in latchet or punch and the balance of the square in flat stitches.

Colors and Stitches:

/   Gold Continental No. 1
| Gold Continental No. 1
Background—Dark Red Broken Cane
   —Design on Charcoal Ground—
Continental No. 1
See Fig. 150 for Cane Design.

For the
Children's Room

Plate 47. Small Butterfly and Flower (see Figs. 100 and 136). These two simple designs combine to form an attractive rug that would be treasured by any child. The background in the flower squares has been enhanced by the imaginative use of the Scotch and Continental stitches.

Small Butterfly
Figs. 99, 100, and Plate 48

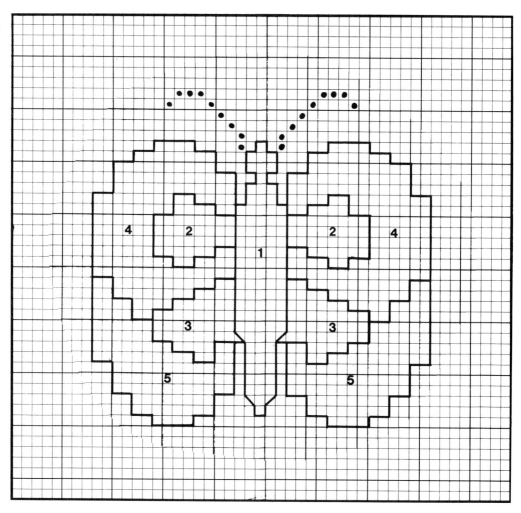

FIG. 99

FIG. 100

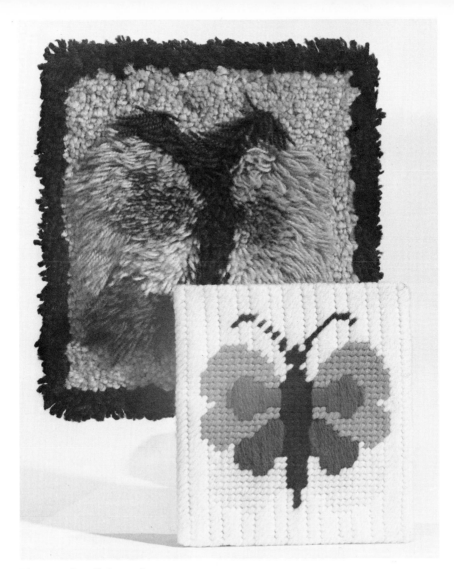

Plate 48. Small Butterfly.
   Other Stitch Suggestions:
      1. Work the entire square in latchet, punch, or rya.
      2. Work the butterfly in latchet or punch and the background in flat stitches.

Colors and Flat Stitches:

●   Black Continental No. 1
1   Black Continental No. 1
2   Red Vertical Satin
3   Dark Blue Vertical Satin
4   Orange Continental No. 1
5   Yellow Continental No. 1
Background—Alternate rows of Eggshell—Flat Stem Nos. 1 and 5

Rya and Latchet Colors:

●   Plum Rya
1   Plum Rya
2   Lavender Rya
3   Pink Rya
4   Light Blue Rya
5   Dark Blue Rya
Background—Pink Latchet
Border—Three rows of Brown Latchet

Owl with Flowers
Figs. 101, 102, and Plate 49

FIG. 101

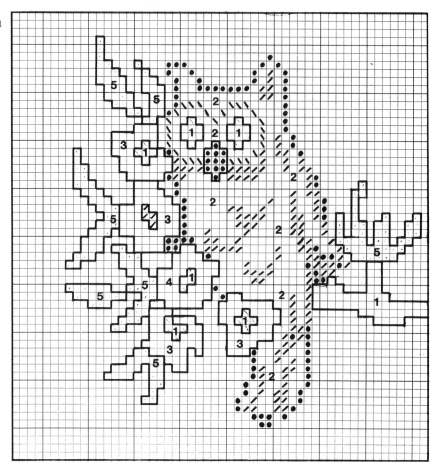

FIG. 102

Plate 49. *Owl with Flowers.*
   Other Stitch Suggestions:
      1. Work the entire square in latchet or punch.
      2. Work the design in latchet or punch and the background in flat stitches.

Colors and Stitches:

- Medium Brown Continental No. 1
/ Dark Turquoise Continental No. 1
\ Black Continental No. 1
1 Black Continental No. 1

2 Tan Mosaic No. 1
3 Light Turquoise Diagonal Satin
4 Dark Turquoise Diagonal Satin
5 Green Continental No. 1
Background—Gold Mosaic No. 1
Border—Medium Brown Mosaic No. 1

119

Japanese Girl
Figs. 103, 104, and Plate 50

FIG. 103

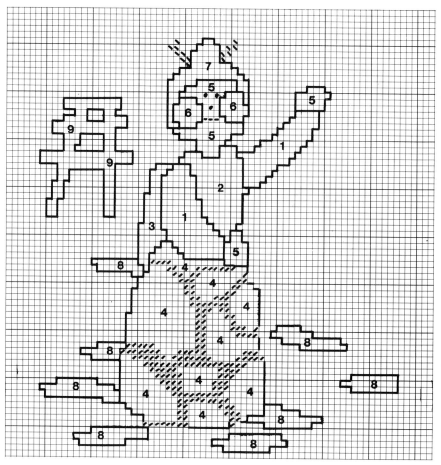

FIG. 104

Plate 50. Japanese Girl. Executed by Ronald Wentz.
  Other Stitch Suggestions:
    1. Work the entire square in latchet, punch, or rya.
    2. Work the girl in latchet or punch and the balance of the square in flat stitches.

Colors and Stitches:

1	Dark Blue Continental No. 1		7	Black Continental No. 1
2	Yellow Continental No. 1		8	Tan Continental No. 1
3	Red Continental No. 1		9	Orange Continental No. 1
4	Light Blue Continental No. 1		/	Dark Blue Continental No. 1
5	Eggshell Continental No. 1		\	Red Continental No. 1
6	Pink Continental No. 1		●	Black Continental No. 1
			--	Red Continental No. 1

Background—Light Blue Scotch No. 1

121

Scattered Mushrooms
Figs. 105, 106, and Plate 51

FIG. 105

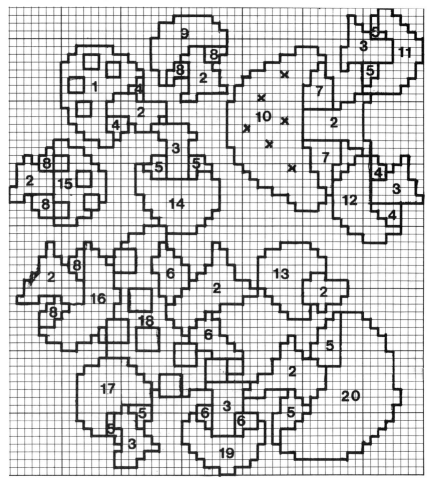

FIG. 106

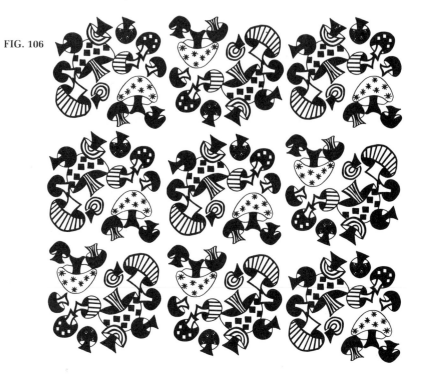

Plate 51. Scattered Mushrooms. Executed by Sue Jane Wentz.
Other Stitch Suggestions:
1. Work the entire square in latchet.
2. Work the mushrooms in latchet and the background in flat stitches.

Colors and Stitches:

1 Medium Purple Continental No. 1 with Gold and Red Double Cross
2 Medium Green Continental No. 1
3 Dark Green Continental No. 1
4 Dark Purple Continental No. 1
5 Dark Blue Continental No. 1
6 Medium Blue Continental No. 1
7 Dark Brown Continental No. 1
8 Medium Brown Continental No. 1
9 Alternate rows of Light Yellow and Orange/Gold Flat Stem No. 1
10 Orange Continental No. 1 with Blue and Light Yellow Double Cross
11 Crescent-shaped rows of shades of Blue and Turquoise Continental No. 1
12 Alternate rows of Medium Blue and Medium Purple Flat Stem No. 3

13 Alternate rows of Dark Gold and Red Diagonal Mosaic No. 1
14 Crescent-shaped rows of Yellow, Orange, and Blue Continental No. 1
15 Light Yellow Continental with Light Blue Mosaic No. 1
16 Crescent-shaped rows of Gold, Brown, Rust, and Yellow Continental No. 1
17 Alternate rows of Dark Red and Light Blue Flat Stem No. 1
18 Medium Purple Continental No. 1 and Turquoise Scotch No. 1
19 Alternate rows of Yellow and Medium Blue Continental No. 1
20 Alternate rows of Medium Blue and Medium Purple Flat Stem No. 3

Background—Gold Continental No. 1

Czech Girl
Figs. 107, 108, and Plate 52

FIG. 107

FIG. 108

Plate 52. Czech Girl.
   Other Stitch Suggestions:
     1. Work the entire square in latchet, punch, or rya.
     2. Work the girl in latchet or punch and the balance of the square in flat stitches.

Colors and Stitches:

1	Peach Continental No. 1
2	Orange Continental No. 1
3	Red Continental No. 1
4	Light Green Continental No. 1
5	Dark Blue Continental No. 1
6	Gold Continental No. 1
7	White Continental No. 1
8	Black Continental No. 1

9	Pink Continental No. 1
10	Medium Green Continental No. 1
●	Dark Blue Continental No. 1
/	Gold Continental No. 1
I	Black Continental No. 1
-	Red Continental No. 1
+	Light Blue Continental No. 1

Background—Light Blue Scotch No. 1
    and Medium Blue Continental No. 1

Whimsical Lion

Figs. 109, 110, and Plate 53

FIG. 109

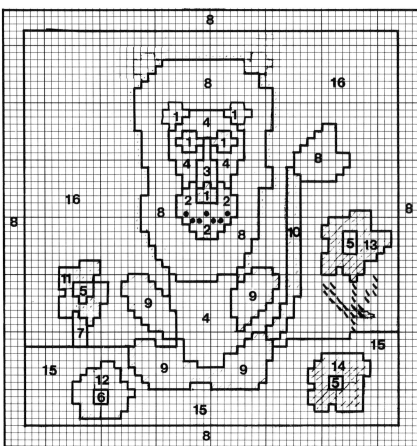

FIG. 110

Plate 53. Whimsical Lion.
   Other Stitch Suggestions:
      1. Work the entire square in latchet, punch, or rya.
      2. Work the lion in rya and the balance of the square in latchet.
      3. Work the lion, flowers, stems, and leaves in latchet or punch and the balance of
      the square in flat stitches.

Colors and Stitches:

\	Light Green Continental No. 1	7	Light Green Flat Stem No. 2
●	Black Continental No. 1	8	Gold Punch
1	Black Continental No. 1	9	Gold Web No. 1
2	Eggshell Web No. 1	10	Gold Continental No. 1
3	Red Continental No. 1	11	Pink Diagonal Satin
4	Yellow Continental No. 1	12	Light Orange Diagonal Satin
5	Red Continental No. 1	13	Dark Orange Diagonal Satin
6	Pink Continental No. 1	14	Blue Diagonal Satin
		15	Dark Green Punch
		16	Tan Mosaic No. 1

Miss U.S.A.
Figs. 111, 112, and Plate 54

FIG. 111

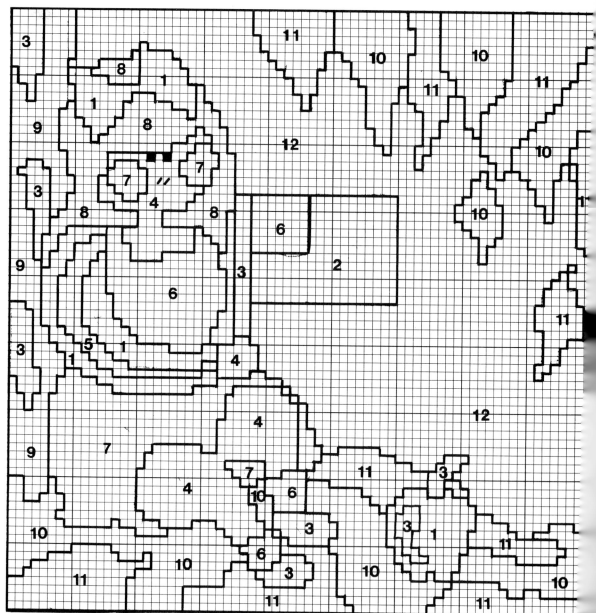

FIG. 112

Plate 54. Miss U.S.A.
   Other Stitch Suggestions:
      1. Work the entire square in latchet, punch, or rya.
      2. Work the girl, grass, apple, and tree trunk in latchet or punch and the balance of the square in flat stitches.

Colors and Stitches:

- ■ Black Continental No. 1
- 1 Red Continental No. 1
- 2 Red and White Stripes   Continental No. 1
- 3 Black Continental No. 1
- 4 Eggshell Continental No. 1

- 5 White Continental No. 1
- 6 Light Blue Continental No. 1
- 7 Pink Continental No. 1
- 8 Yellow Continental No. 1
- 9 Rust Continental No. 1
- 10 Dark Green Continental No. 1
- 11 Light Green Continental No. 1
- 12 Tan Continental No. 1

Sailboat
Figs. 113, 114, and Plate 55

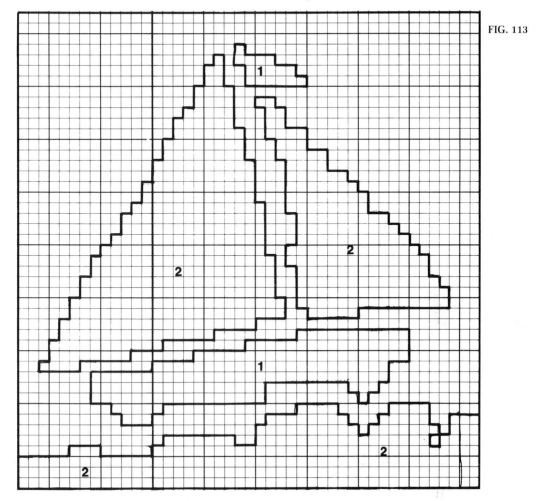

FIG. 113

FIG. 114

131

Plate 55. Sailboat.
    Other Stitch Suggestions:
        1. Work the entire square in latchet, punch, or rya.
        2. Work the boat and waves in rya and the background in latchet.
        3. Work the boat and waves in latchet or punch and the background in flat stitches.

Colors and Stitches:

    1   Red Continental No. 1
    2   Blue Continental No. 1
    Background—White Continental No. 1

Anchor and Stars
Figs. 115, 116, and Plate 56

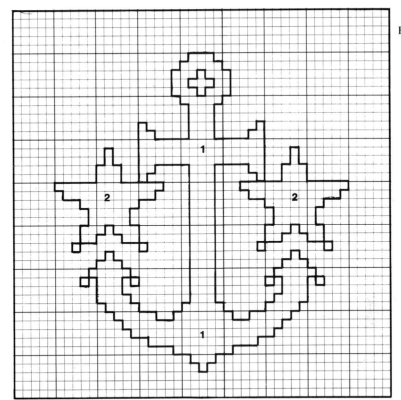

FIG. 115

FIG. 116

Plate 56. Anchor and Stars. Executed by Ronald Wentz.
Other Stitch Suggestions:
1. Work the entire square in latchet, punch, or rya.
2. Work the anchor and stars in rya and the background in latchet.
3. Work the anchor and stars in latchet and the background in flat stitches.

Colors and Flat Stitches:

1 Red Continental No. 1
2 Blue Continental No. 1

Background—White Diagonal Mosaic—
No. 1

For the Bathroom

Plate 57. Graphic Double V (see Fig. 122). Worked as a small bathroom rug, this design could be easily expanded to fit any size room. The flat stem stitches fit perfectly into the diamond areas. The punch areas serve to accent each of the diamonds and add an interesting texture.

Graphic V
Figs. 117, 118, and Plate 58

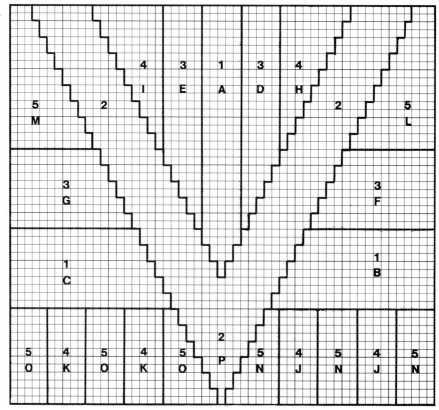

FIG. 117

FIG. 118

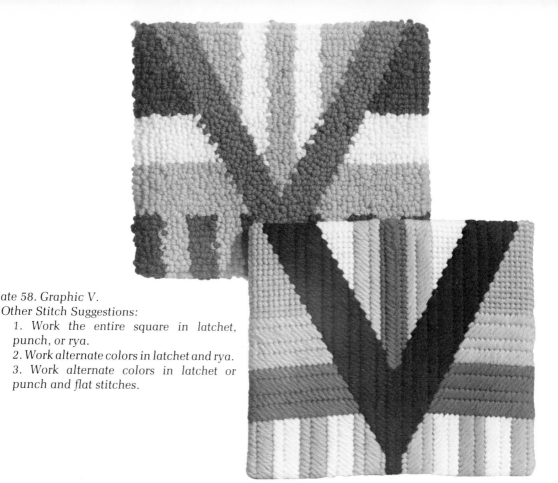

Plate 58. Graphic V.
Other Stitch Suggestions:
1. Work the entire square in latchet, punch, or rya.
2. Work alternate colors in latchet and rya.
3. Work alternate colors in latchet or punch and flat stitches.

Colors and Flat Stitches:

A One row of Red Fern down the center, one row of Red Continental No. 1 on the right side and one row of Red Continental No. 2 on the left side.
B Alternate rows of Red Flat Stem Nos. 3 and 7
C Alternate rows of Red Flat Stem Nos. 4 and 8
D Orange Flat Stem Nos. 1 and 5
E Orange Flat Stem Nos. 2 and 6
F Alternate rows of Orange Flat Stem Nos. 3 and 7
G Alternate rows of Orange Flat Stem Nos. 4 and 8
H Yellow Continental No. 1
I Yellow Continental No. 2
J Alternate rows of Yellow Flat Stem Nos. 1 and 5
K Alternate rows of Yellow Flat Stem Nos. 2 and 6

L Salmon Continental No. 1
M Salmon Continental No. 2
N Alternate rows of Salmon Flat Stem Nos. 1 and 5
O Alternate rows of Salmon Flat Stem Nos. 2 and 6
P One row of Brown Fern at the bottom center of the "V" with alternate rows of Brown Flat Stem Nos. 1 and 5 on the right side and alternate rows of Brown Flat Stem Nos. 2 and 6 on the left side

Punch Colors:

1 Pink
2 Red
3 Yellow
4 Orange
5 Dark Blue

137

Diamond

Figs. 119, 120, and Plate 59

FIG. 119

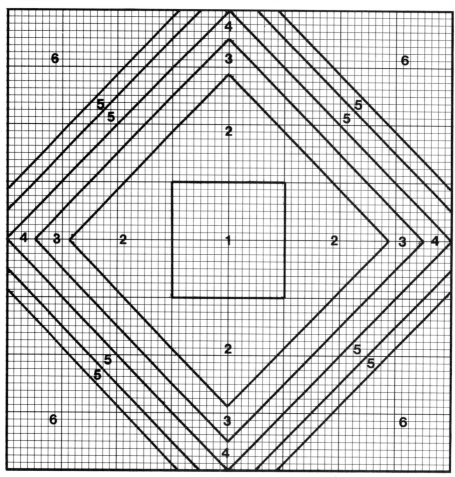

FIG. 120

Plate 59. Diamond.

Other Stitch Suggestions:

1. Work the entire square in latchet, punch, or rya.
2. Work the diamonds and square in the center in rya and the corners in latchet.
3. Work the diamonds and square in the center in latchet or punch and the corners in flat stitches.
4. Work the square in the center and the light blue diamond in rya, the diamond bands in latchet, and the corners in flat stitches.

Colors and Stitches:

1 Yellow Vertical Satin covering four threads
2 Light Blue Continental No. 1
3 Dark Blue Vertical Satin
4 Light Yellow Continental No. 1
5 Light Blue Vertical Satin
6 Dark Blue Continental No. 1

Graphic Double V
Figs. 121, 122, and Plate 60

FIG. 121

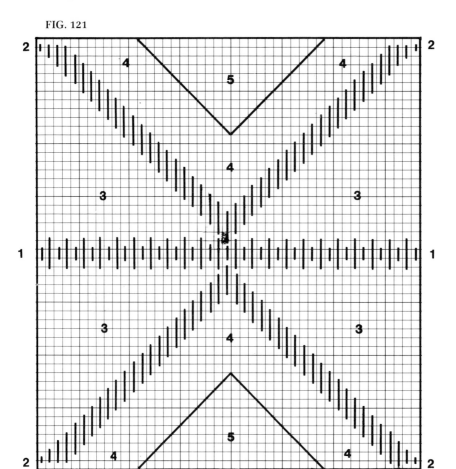

FIG. 122

Plate 60. Graphic Double V.
  Other Stitch Suggestions:
    1. Work the entire square in latchet, punch, or rya.
    2. Work the double "V's" in rya and the balance of the square in latchet or flat stitches.
    3. Work the double "V's" in latchet or punch and the balance of the square in flat stitches.
    4. See Plate 57 for another combination of punch and flat stitches.

Colors and Stitches:

1 Red Vertical Satin
2 Pink Vertical Satin
3 Orange Vertical Satin
4 Red Continental No. 1
5 Orange Continental No. 1

Squares and Crescents
Figs. 123, 124, and Plate 61

FIG. 123

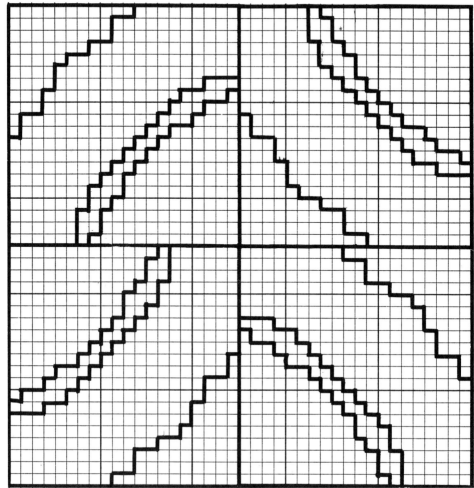

FIG. 124

142

Plate 61. Squares and Crescents. Executed by Grace Gitt Wentz.
   Other Stitch Suggestions:
      1. Work the entire square in latchet, punch, or rya.
      2. Work alternate squares in latchet and rya.
      3. Work alternate squares in punch and flat stitches or latchet and flat stitches.

Colors and Stitches:

The entire design is worked in Continental No. 1 in Blue, Green, Orange, and Eggshell. The design is turned in different directions for each square.

Grid Design
Figs. 125, 126, and Plate 62

FIG. 125

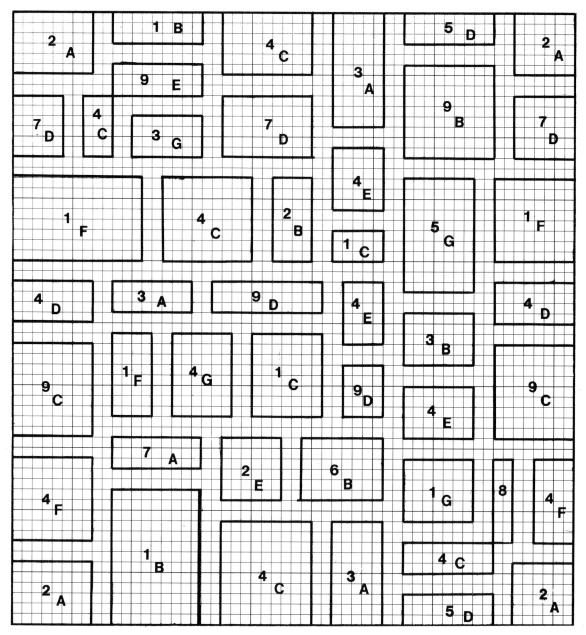

FIG. 126

145

Plate 62. Grid Design.
   Other Stitch Suggestions:
      1. Work the entire square in punch, rya, or flat stitches.
      2. Work random squares in rya and punch.
      3. Work the bands in rya and the squares in latchet.

Colors and Flat Stitches:

1 Yellow Punch
2 Gold Mosaic No. 1
3 Gold Continental No. 1
4 Orange Diagonal Mosaic No. 1
5 Tan Continental No. 1
6 Tan Mosaic No. 1
7 Tan Flat Stem No. 2
8 Tan Flat Stem No. 1
9 Rust Web No. 1
Unmarked Bands are worked in Olive/
   Brown, Flat Stem Nos. 1 and 3

Latchet Colors:

A Medium Gold
B Dark Brown
C Dark Orange
D Light Gold
E Yellow/Orange
F Light Yellow
G Dark Gold

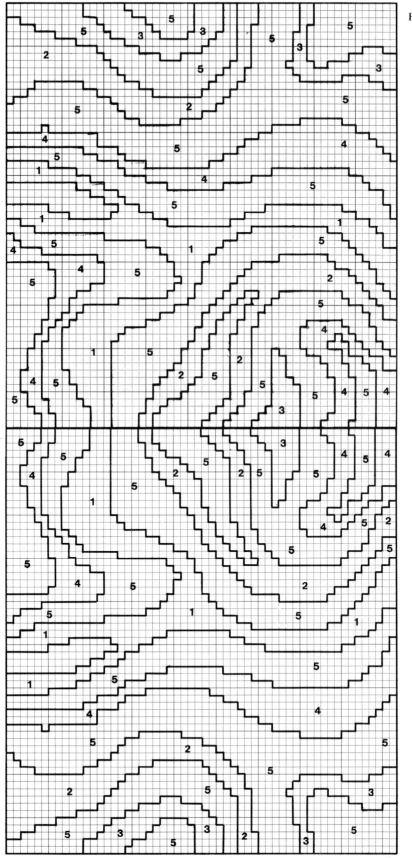

FIG. 127

FIG. 128

Plate 63. Waves.
   Other Stitch Suggestions:
      1. Work the entire square in latchet, punch, or rya.
      2. Work alternate bands in rya and latchet.
      3. Work alternate bands in latchet and flat stitches.
      4. Work alternate bands in punch and flat stitches.

Colors and Stitches:

1 Bright Pink Web No. 1
2 Salmon Web No. 1

3 Orange Web No. 1
4 Gold Web No. 1
5 Light Pink Web No. 1

Seashell

Figs. 129, 130, and Plate 64

FIG. 129

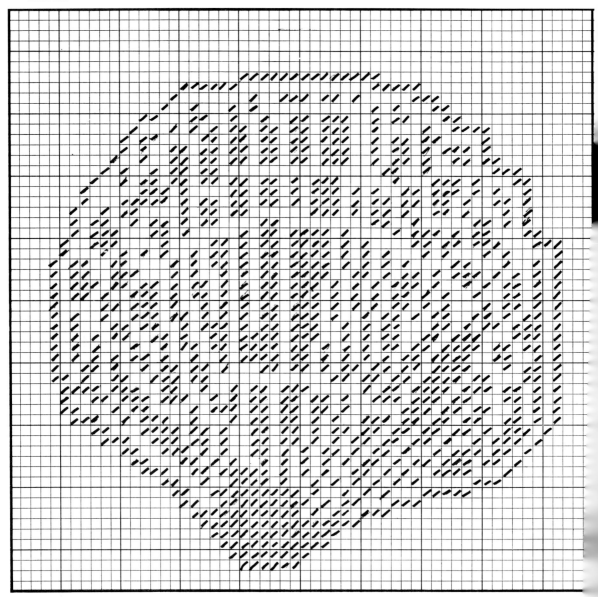

FIG. 130

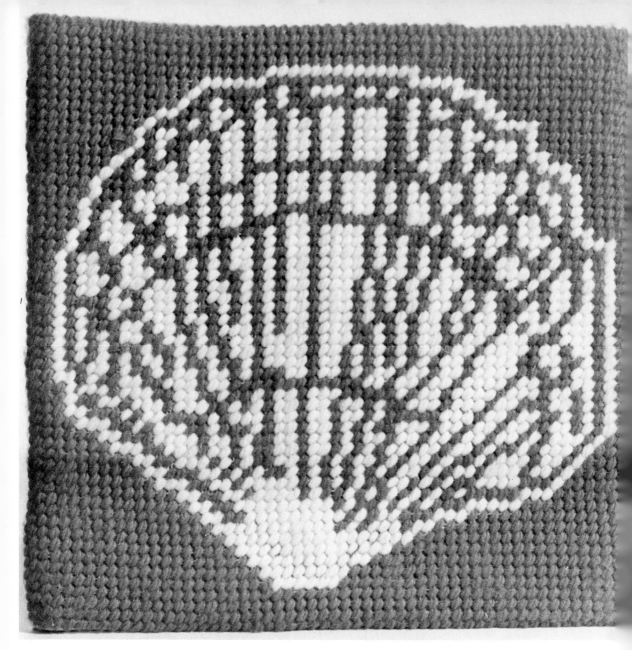

Plate 64. Seashell.
Other Stitch Suggestions:
1. Work the entire square in latchet, punch, or rya.
2. Work the shell in rya and the background in latchet.
3. Work the shell in latchet or punch and the background in flat stitches.

Colors and Stitches:

/ White Continental No. 1
The balance of the inside of the shell
and the background are worked in
Medium Blue Continental No. 1.

152

Small Flowers
Figs. 131, 132, and Plate 65

FIG. 131

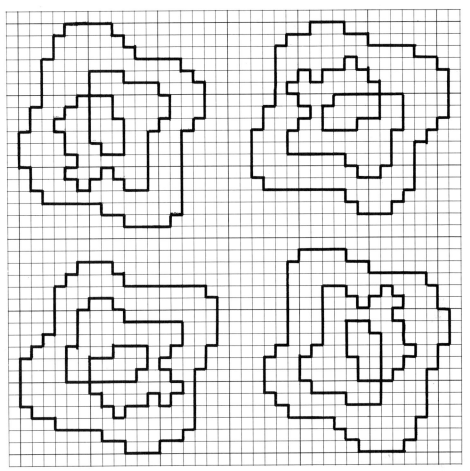

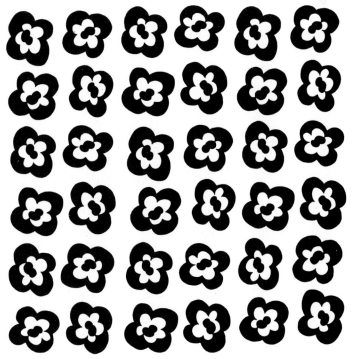

FIG. 132

Plate 65. Small Flowers. Executed by Ronald Wentz.
   Other Stitch Suggestions:
      1. Work the entire square in latchet or rya.
      2. Work the flowers in rya and the background in latchet.
      3. Work the flowers in latchet or punch and the background in flat stitches.
      4. Work the two center areas of each flower in rya, the outside area of each flower in latchet, and the background in flat stitches.

Colors and Flat Stitches:

Alternate the flowers in shades of Rose and shades of Blue Continental No. 1 —Background—Alternate Light and Medium Olive Mosaic No. 1

Punch Colors:

Alternate the flowers in Pink/Red/ Orange and Orange/Yellow/Red. Background—Eggshell

Tile Number Four

Figs. 133, 134, and Plate 66

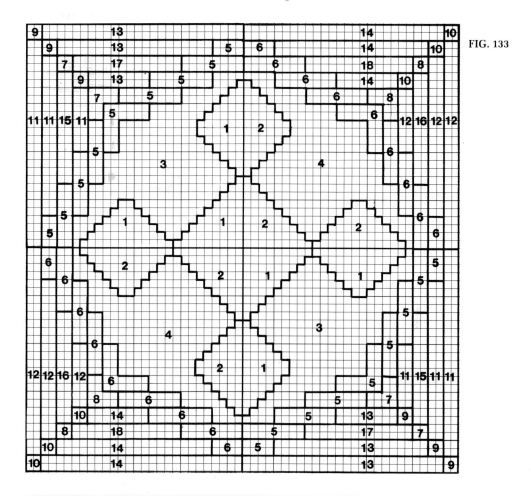

FIG. 133

FIG. 134

155

Plate 66. Tile Number Four.
Other Stitch Suggestions:
    1. Work the entire square in latchet, punch, or rya.
    2. Work the circle in rya and the balance of the square in latchet.
    3. Work the circle in latchet or punch and the balance of the design in flat stitches.
    4. Work the five diamonds in rya, the balance of the circle in latchet, and the outside corners and border in flat stitches.

Colors and Stitches:

1 Dark Blue Continental No. 1	8 Olive Mosaic No. 2
2 Dark Blue Continental No. 2	9 Light Blue Mosaic No. 1
3 Alternate White and Black Diagonal Mosaic No. 1	10 Light Blue Mosaic No. 2
4 Alternate White and Black Diagonal Mosaic No. 2	11 Light Blue Flat Stem No. 1
5 Dark Blue Mosaic No. 1	12 Light Blue Flat Stem No. 2
6 Dark Blue Mosaic No. 2	13 Light Blue Flat Stem No. 3
7 Olive Mosaic No. 1	14 Light Blue Flat Stem No. 4
	15 Olive Flat Stem No. 1
	16 Olive Flat Stem No. 2
	17 Olive Flat Stem No. 3
	18 Olive Flat Stem No. 4

For the Sunroom

Plate 67. Paisley Rug (see Figs. 141, 142, and 143).

Flowers and Stripes

Figs. 135, 136, and Plate 68

FIG. 135

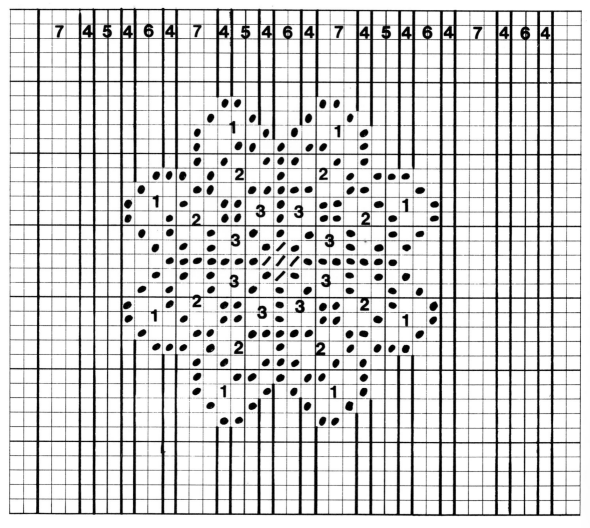

FIG. 136

Plate 68. Flowers and Stripes.
   Other Stitch Suggestions:
      1. Work the entire square in latchet, punch, or rya.
      2. Work the flowers in rya and the background in latchet.
      3. Work the flowers in rya and the background in alternate rows of latchet and rya.
      4. Work the flowers in latchet or punch and the background in flat stitches.

Colors and Stitches:

●   Navy Continental No. 1
/, 1, 2, and 3 worked in Continental No. 1.
The flowers are worked in Pink, Rose, Lavender and Red, each flower being worked in a different color sequence.

The background is worked in stripes of varying shades of green in the following stitches:

4   Continental No. 1
5   Mosaic No. 1
6   Flat Stem No. 1
7   Flat Stem No. 5

FIG. 138

Plate 69. Giant Butterfly.

Other Stitch Suggestions:

1. Work the entire square in latchet, punch, or rya.
2. Work the butterfly in rya and the background in latchet.
3. Work the butterfly in latchet or punch and the background in flat stitches.

Colors and Flat Stitches:

- ♦   Navy Continental No. 1
- ♦   Navy Continental No. 2
- 1   Orange Continental No. 1
- 2   Orange Continental No. 2
- 3   Yellow Continental No. 1
- 4   Yellow Continental No. 2
- 5   Red Continental No. 1
- 6   Red Continental No. 2
- 7   Navy Vertical Satin
- 8   Navy Fern
- 9   Blue Vertical Satin
- 10   Red Vertical Satin
- 11   Yellow Horizontal Satin
- 12   Eggshell Continental No. 1
- 13   Eggshell Continental No. 2
- 14   Blue Vertical Satin

Rya Colors:

- ♦, ♦, and 8   Gray
- 7   Black
- 1 and 2   Medium Blue
- 10   Plum
- 5 and 6   Dark Blue
- 9 and 11   Red
- 14   Yellow
- 1, 2, 3, and 4   Gold
- 12   Green Diagonal Mosaic No. 1
- 13   Green Diagonal Mosaic No. 2

Daisies

Figs. 139, 140, and Plate 70

FIG. 139

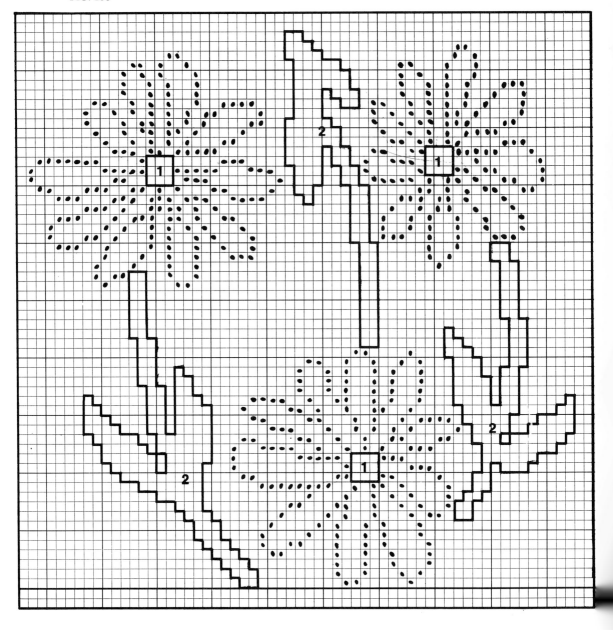

FIG. 140

Plate 70. Daisies.

Other Stitch Suggestions:

1. Work the entire square in latchet, punch, or rya.

2. Work the daisies and stems in rya and the background in latchet.

3. Work the daisies in latchet and the balance of the square in flat stitches.

Colors and Stitches:

● Light Yellow Punch
Fill in petals with Medium Orange Punch

1 Rust Punch
2 Medium Green Continental No. 1
Background—Brown/Olive Continental No. 1

166

Paisley Rug
Figs. 141, 142, 143, and Plate 67

Plate 67. Paisley Rug (see Figs. 141, 142, and 143).
   Other Stitch Suggestions:
      1. Work the entire square in latchet, punch, or rya.
      2. Work the design in rya and the background in latchet.
      3. Work the design in latchet or punch and the background in flat stitches.
      4. Work alternate sections of the design in latchet and rya and the background in flat stitches.

Colors and Stitches:

1 Pink Diagonal Gobelin No. 1
2 Red Diagonal Gobelin No. 1
3 Rose Diagonal Gobelin No. 1
4 Purple Diagonal Gobelin No. 1

5 Green Diagonal Gobelin No. 1
6 Orange Diagonal Gobelin No. 1
7 Navy Diagonal Gobelin No. 1
Background—Eggshell Diagonal Gobelin No. 1

FIG. 141   FIG. 142

FIG. 143

FIG. 143

Bee
Figs. 144, 145, and Plate 71

FIG. 144

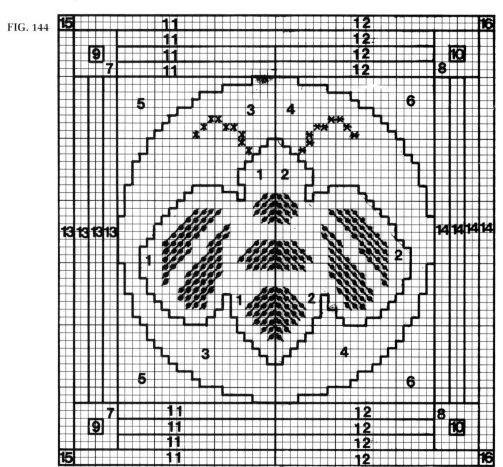

FIG. 145

170

Plate 71. Bee.

Other Stitch Suggestions:

    1. Work the entire square in latchet, punch, or rya.

    2. Work the bee and circle in rya and the balance of the square in latchet.

    3. Work the bee and circle in latchet or punch and the balance of the square in flat stitches.

    4. Work the bee in rya, the circle in latchet, and the balance of the square in flat stitches.

Colors and Stitches:

1	Brown Continental No. 1	11	Brown Flat Stem No. 3
2	Brown Continental No. 2	12	Brown Flat Stem No. 4
3	Light Blue Continental No. 1	13	Brown Flat Stem No. 1
4	Light Blue Continental No. 2	14	Brown Flat Stem No. 2
5	Dark Olive Mosaic No. 1	15	Brown Mosaic No. 1
6	Dark Olive Mosaic No. 2	16	Brown Mosaic No. 2
7	Medium Olive Mosaic No. 1	✦	Dark Blue Flat Stem No. 1
8	Medium Olive Mosaic No. 2	✦	Dark Blue Flat Stem No. 2
9	Dark Blue Mosaic No. 1	✷	Brown Continental No. 1
10	Dark Blue Mosaic No. 2	✷	Brown Continental No. 2

Tile Number Five
Figs. 146, 147, and Plate 72

FIG. 146

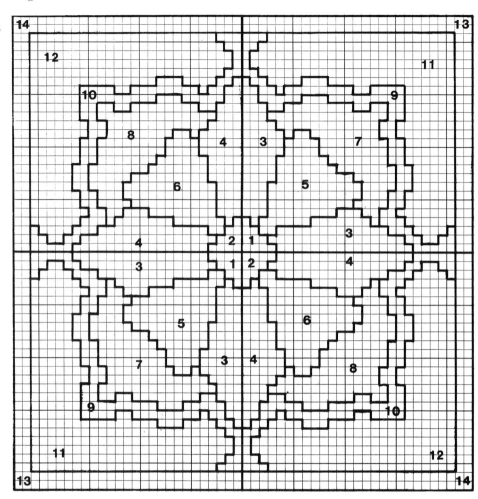

FIG. 147

Plate 72. Tile Number Five.
  Other Stitch Suggestions:
    1. Work the entire square in latchet, punch, or rya.
    2. Work the center motif in rya and the brown and eggshell in latchet.
    3. Work the center motif in latchet, punch, or rya and the brown and eggshell in flat stitches.

Colors and Stitches:

1	Red Continental No. 1
2	Red Continental No. 2
3	Salmon Continental No. 1
4	Salmon Continental No. 2
5	Maroon Continental No. 1
6	Maroon Continental No. 2
7	Orange Continental No. 1
8	Orange Continental No. 2
9	Brown Continental No. 1
10	Brown Continental No. 2
11	Eggshell Flat Stem Nos. 1 and 3
12	Eggshell Flat Stem Nos. 2 and 4
13	Brown Flat Stem Nos. 1 and 3
14	Brown Flat Stem Nos. 2 and 4

Rose on Broken Cane

Figs. 148, 149, 150, and Plate 73

FIG. 148

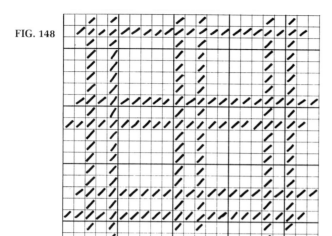

FIG. 149

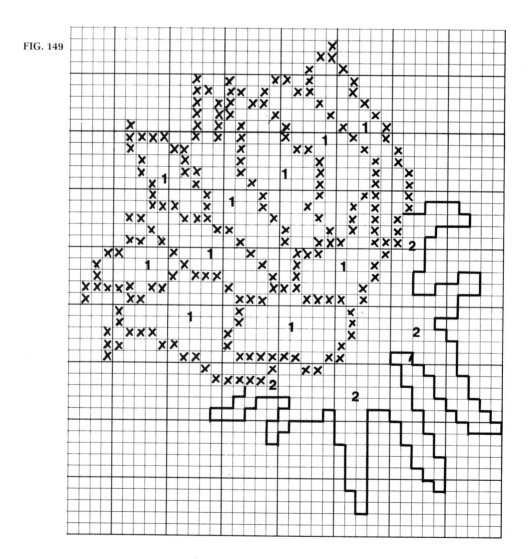

FIG. 150

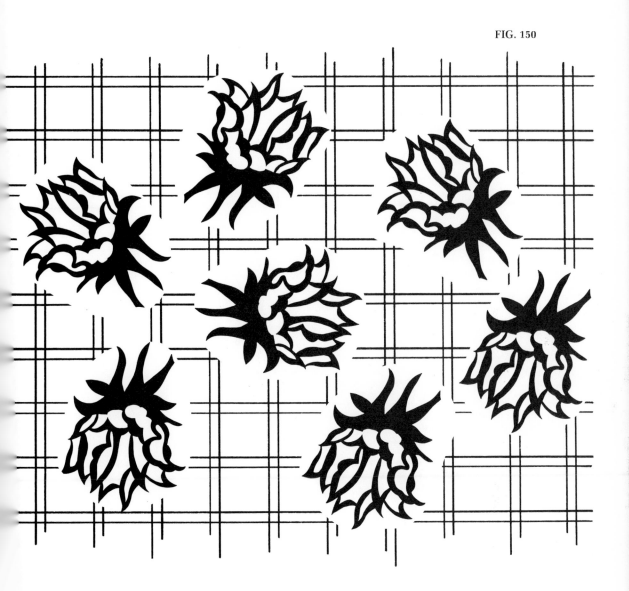

Colors and Stitches:

1 Medium Rose Diagonal Mosaic No. 1
2 Green Continental No. 1

/ Medium Brown Continental No. 1
× Dark Rose Continental No. 1
Background—Tan Continental No. 1
Cane pattern should stop before touching rose, as if broken.

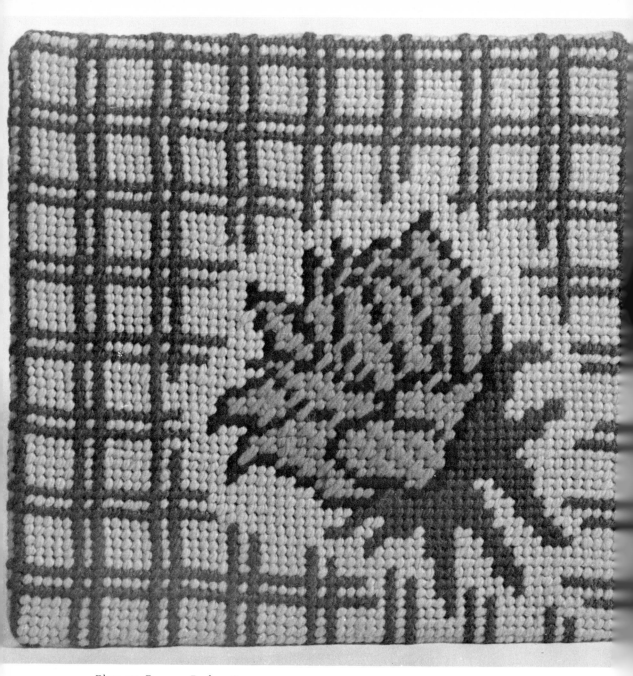

Plate 73. Rose on Broken Cane.
  Other Stitch Suggestions:
    1. Work the entire square in latchet, punch, or rya.
    2. Work the rose in rya and the balance of the square in latchet.
    3. Work the rose in latchet or punch and the balance of the square in flat stitches.

176

FIG. 151

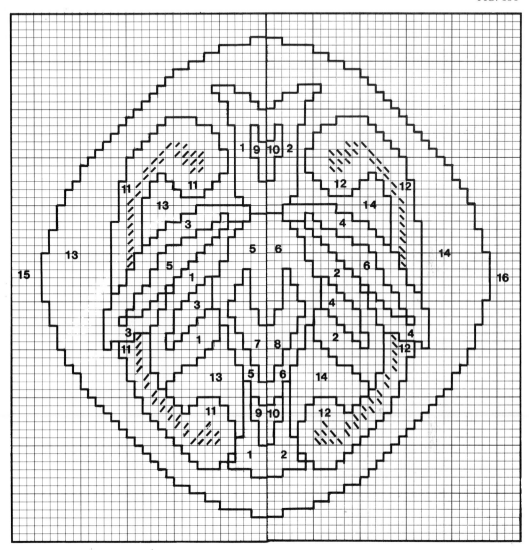

FIG. 152

Plate 74. Bamboo Fan.
   Other Stitch Suggestions:
      1. Work the entire square in latchet, punch, or rya.
      2. Work the bamboo fan and circle in rya and the balance of the square in latchet.
      3. Work the bamboo fan and circle in latchet or punch and the balance of the square in flat stitches.
      4. Work the bamboo fan in rya, the circle in latchet, and the balance of the square in flat stitches.

Colors and Stitches:

1	Dark Blue Continental No. 1
2	Dark Blue Continental No. 2
3	Light Blue Continental No. 1
4	Light Blue Continental No. 2
5	Medium Blue Continental No. 1
6	Medium Blue Continental No. 2
7	Blue/Gray Continental No. 1
8	Blue/Gray Continental No. 2
9	Tan Continental No. 1
10	Tan Continental No. 2
11	Medium Gold Continental No. 1
12	Medium Gold Continental No. 2
13	Eggshell Diagonal Mosaic No. 1
14	Eggshell Diagonal Mosaic No. 2
15	Olive Scotch No. 1
16	Olive Scotch No. 2
/	Light Gold Continental No. 1
\	Light Gold Continental No. 2

179

Bamboo with Tassels

Figs. 153, 154, and Plate 75

FIG. 153

180

FIG. 154

Plate 75. Bamboo with Tassels.
Other Stitch Suggestions:
    1. Work the entire square in latchet, punch, or rya.
    2. Work the bamboo and circle in rya and the balance of the square in latchet.
    3. Work the bamboo and circle in punch and the balance of the square in flat stitches.
    4. Work the bamboo in rya, the circle in latchet, and the balance of the square in flat stitches.

Colors and Flat Stitches:

  1 Gold Continental No. 1
  2 Gold Continental No. 2
  3 Light Blue Continental No. 1
  4 Light Blue Continental No. 2
  5 Medium Blue Continental No. 1
  6 Medium Blue Continental No. 2
  7 Dark Blue Continental No. 1
  8 Dark Blue Continental No. 2
  9 Blue/Gray Continental No. 1
10 Blue/Gray Continental No. 2
11 Medium Olive Flat Stem No. 1
12 Medium Olive Flat Stem No. 2
13 Medium Olive Flat Stem No. 5
14 Medium Olive Flat Stem No. 6
15 Eggshell Diagonal Mosaic No. 1
16 Eggshell Diagonal Mosaic No. 2
17 Green Scotch No. 1
18 Green Scotch No. 2

19 Light Blue Continental No. 1
20 Light Blue Continental No. 2
21 Medium Blue Continental No. 1
22 Medium Blue Continental No. 2

Latchet Colors:

  1 and 2 Gold
  3 and 4 Medium Green
  5, 6, 9, and 10 Light Blue
  7 and 8 Light Green
19 and 20 Medium Blue
11, 12, 13, and 14 Dark Brown
15 and 16 Eggshell
21 and 22 Olive
17 Medium Brown Diagonal Mosaic No. 2
18 Medium Brown Diagonal Mosaic No. 1

Plate 76. Blazing Star Quilt Design (see Fig. 158). This simple quilt design has been worked into a three-dimensional rug. Each square incorporates rya, latchet, and flat stitches.

Stars and Diamonds Quilt Design
Figs. 155, 156, and Plate 77

FIG. 155

FIG. 156

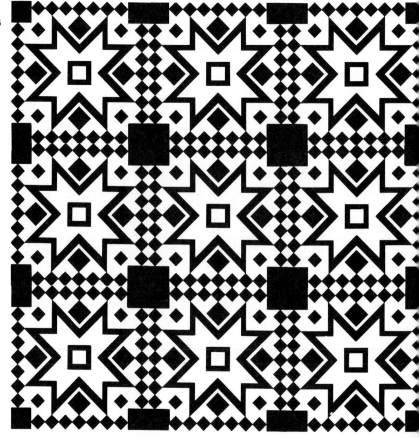

184

Plate 77. Star and Diamonds Quilt Design.
  Other Stitch Suggestions:
    1. Work the entire square in latchet, punch, or rya.
    2. Work the star in rya and the balance of the square in latchet.
    3. Work the star in latchet or punch and the balance of the square in flat stitches.
    4. Work the star in rya, the diamonds in latchet, and the balance of the square in flat stitches.

Colors and Stitches:

1 Light Yellow Straight Cross
2 Dark Brown Straight Cross
3 Medium Yellow Diagonal Mosaic No. 1
4 Medium Yellow Diagonal Mosaic No. 2
5 Dark Brown Diagonal Mosaic No. 1
6 Dark Brown Diagonal Mosaic No. 2
7 Dark Brown Flat Stem No. 1
8 Dark Brown Flat Stem No. 2
9 Dark Brown Flat Stem No. 3
10 Dark Brown Flat Stem No. 4
11 Dark Brown Mosaic No. 1
12 Dark Brown Mosaic No. 2
13 Medium Orange Straight Cross
14 Light Orange Straight Cross
15 Medium Brown Diagonal Mosaic No. 1
16 Medium Brown Diagonal Mosaic No. 2
⊕ Medium Orange Straight Cross

Blazing Star Quilt Design

Figs. 157, 158, and Plate 78

FIG. 157

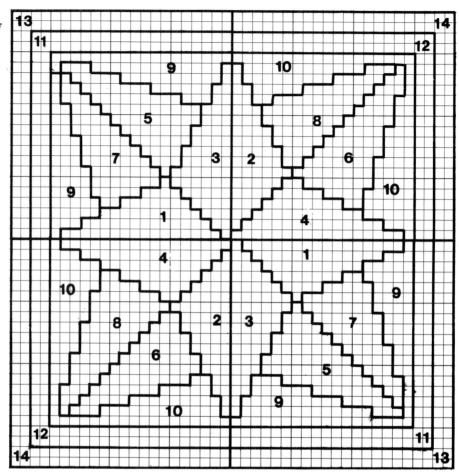

FIG. 158

186

Plate 78. Blazing Star Quilt Design.
Other Stitch Suggestions:

    1. Work the entire square in latchet or rya.

    2. Work all eight points of the star in rya and the balance of the square in latchet.

    3. Work all eight points of the star in latchet or punch and the balance of the square in flat stitches.

    4. Work the four center points of the star in rya, the four outside points of the star in latchet, and the balance of the square in flat stitches.

Colors and Flat Stitches:

1   Pink Continental No. 1
2   Pink Continental No. 2
3   Maroon Web No. 1
4   Maroon Web No. 2
5   Light Blue Continental No. 1
6   Light Blue Continental No. 2
7   Medium Blue Diagonal Mosaic No. 1
8   Medium Blue Diagonal Mosaic No. 2
9   Eggshell Continental No. 1
10 Eggshell Continental No. 2

11 Red Mosaic No. 1
12 Red Mosaic No. 2
13 Pink Mosaic No. 1
14 Pink Mosaic No. 2

Punch Colors:

1 and 2   Gold
3 and 4   Brown
5 and 6   Light Blue
7 and 8   Dark Blue
9 and 10 Eggshell
11 and 12 Dark Green
13 and 14 Light Green

Tile Number Six
Figs. 159, 160, and Plate 79

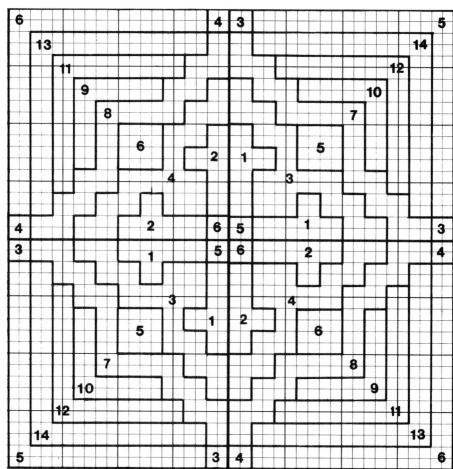

FIG. 159

FIG. 160

Plate 79. Tile Number Six.

Other Stitch Suggestions:

1. Work the entire square in latchet, punch, or rya.

2. Work alternate areas of color in latchet and rya.

3. Work the three center colors in rya, the next two colors from the center in latchet, and the balance of the square in flat stitches.

4. Work the five center colors in latchet or punch and the balance of the square in flat stitches.

Colors and Stitches:

1 Light Orange Mosaic No. 1
2 Light Orange Mosaic No. 2
3 Medium Brown Mosaic No. 1
4 Medium Brown Mosaic No. 2
5 Dark Orange Continental No. 1
6 Dark Orange Continental No. 2
7 Yellow Mosaic No. 1
8 Yellow Mosaic No. 2

9 Medium Orange Flat Stem Nos. 2 and 4
10 Medium Orange Flat Stem Nos. 1 and 3
11 Eggshell Flat Stem Nos. 2 and 4
12 Eggshell Flat Stem Nos. 1 and 3
13 Medium Brown Flat Stem Nos. 2 and 4
14 Medium Brown Flat Stem Nos. 1 and 3

Indian Motif Number Five

Figs. 161, 162, and Plate 80

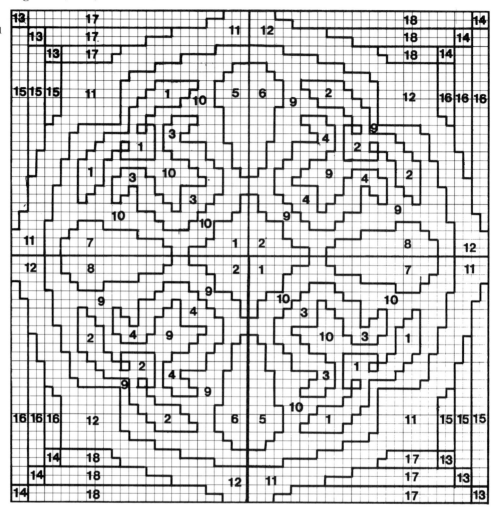

FIG. 161

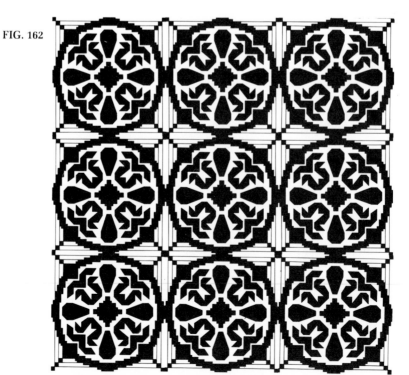

FIG. 162

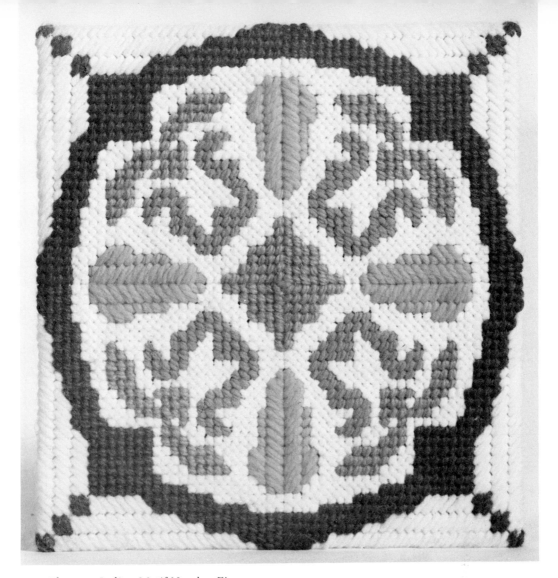

Plate 80. Indian Motif Number Five.
Other Stitch Suggestions:
   1. Work the entire square in latchet, punch, or rya.
   2. Work the colored areas in rya and the background in latchet.
   3. Work the colored areas in latchet or punch and the background in flat stitches.
   4. Work everything within the circle in rya, the circle in latchet and the corners in flat stitches.

Colors and Stitches:

1 Gold Continental No. 1
2 Gold Continental No. 2
3 Medium Orange Continental No. 1
4 Medium Orange Continental No. 2
5 Light Orange Flat Stem No. 1
6 Light Orange Flat Stem No. 2
7 Light Orange Flat Stem No. 3
8 Light Orange Flat Stem No. 4
9 Eggshell Web No. 1
10 Eggshell Web No. 2
11 Brown Continental No. 1
12 Brown Continental No. 2
13 Brown Mosaic No. 1
14 Brown Mosaic No. 2
15 Eggshell Flat Stem No. 1
16 Eggshell Flat Stem No. 2
17 Eggshell Flat Stem No. 3
18 Eggshell Flat Stem No. 4

191

Pears

Figs. 163, 164, and Plate 81

FIG. 163

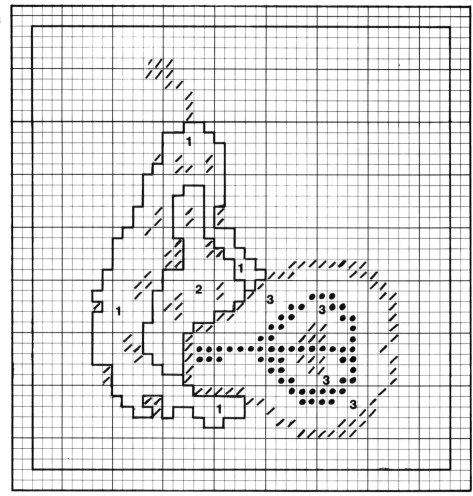

FIG. 164

Plate 81. Pears.
   Other Stitch Suggestions:
      1. Work the entire square in latchet, punch, or rya.
      2. Work the pears in rya and the balance of the square in latchet.
      3. Work the pears in latchet or punch and the balance of the square in flat stitches.

Colors and Stitches:

1 Dark Gold Continental No. 1
2 Light Gold Continental No. 2
3 Eggshell Continental No. 1

/ Tan Continental No. 1
● Black Continental No. 1
Background—Eggshell Mosaic No. 1
Border—Black Flat Stem Nos. 1 and 3

193

Small Sunflowers
Figs. 165, 166, and Plate 82

FIG. 165

FIG. 166

Plate 82. Small Sunflowers. Executed by Ronald Wentz.
Other Stitch Suggestions:
1. Work the entire square in latchet, punch, or rya.
2. Work the flowers in rya and the background in latchet.
3. Work the flowers in latchet or punch and the background in flat stitches.
4. Work the center of the flowers in rya, the petals of the flowers in latchet, and the background in flat stitches.

Colors and Stitches:.

1 Light Peach Diagonal Mosaic No. 1 and Diagonal Satin
2 Medium Peach Diagonal Satin
3 Orange Flat Stem No. 1 and Continental No. 1
4 Orange Flat Stem No. 3 and Continental No. 1
5 Rust Flat Stem No. 1 and Continental No. 1
6 Rust Flat Stem No. 3 and Continental No. 1

7 Dark Gold Flat Stem No. 1 and Continental No. 1
8 Dark Gold Flat Stem No. 3 and Continental No. 1

The other flowers are worked in the same stitches in shades of Yellow and Gold. Flowers may be placed in regular rows across the canvas or may be scattered in a random fashion.

195

Beets

Figs. 167, 168, and Plate 83

FIG. 167

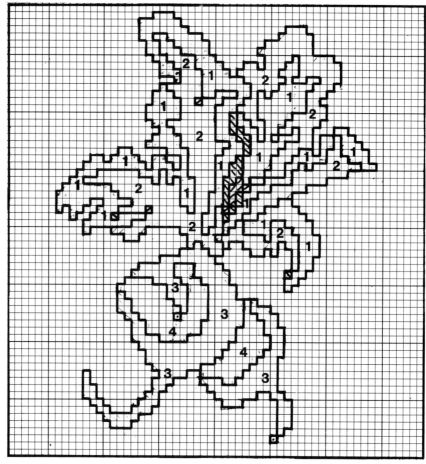

FIG. 168

196

Plate 83. Beets.
  Other Stitch Suggestions:
    1. Work the entire square in latchet, punch, or rya.
    2. Work the beets in rya and the balance of the square in latchet.
    3. Work the beets in latchet or punch and the balance of the square in flat stitches.

Colors and Stitches:

1 Dark Green Continental No. 1
2 Medium Green Continental No. 1
3 Bright Red Continental No. 1
4 Dark Red Web No. 1

/ Dark Green Continental No. 1
\ Medium Green Continental No. 1
● Bright Red Continental No. 1
Background—Eggshell Mosaic No. 1
Border—Brown and Gold Double
  Cross

197

Eggplant
Figs. 169, 170, and Plate 84

FIG. 169

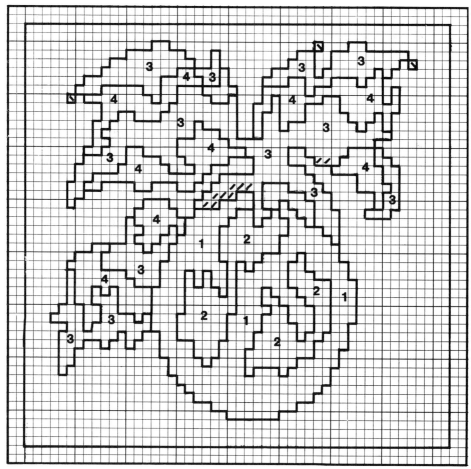

FIG. 170

Plate 84. Eggplant.
   Other Stitch Suggestions:
     1. Work the entire square in latchet or rya.
     2. Work the eggplant in rya and the balance of the square in latchet.
     3. Work the eggplant in latchet or punch and the balance of the square in flat stitches.

Colors and Flat Stitches:

1 Medium Purple Web No. 1
2 Dark Purple Continental No. 1
3 and \ Light Green Web No. 1
4 and / Dark Green Web No. 1
Background—Tan Diagonal Mosaic No. 1
Border—Medium and Dark Purple Double Cross

Punch Colors:

1 Medium Purple
2 Dark Purple
3 and \ Light Green
4 and / Dark Green
Background—Eggshell
Border—Eggshell

199

Four-petaled Flower
Figs. 171, 172, and Plate 85

FIG. 171

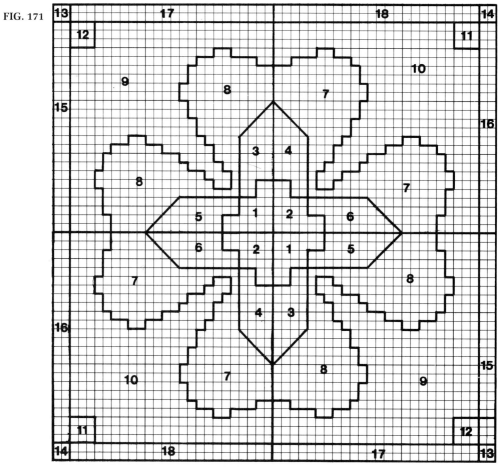

FIG. 172

Plate 85. Four-petaled Flower:
  Other Stitch Suggestions:
    1. Work the entire square in latchet, punch, or rya.
    2. Work the flower in latchet or punch and the balance of the square in flat stitches.
    3. Work the center circle and center of each petal in rya, the outside of each petal in latchet, and the balance of the square in flat stitches.

Colors and Flat Stitches:

  1 Yellow Mosaic No. 1
  2 Yellow Mosaic No. 2
  3 Dark Blue Flat Stem No. 1
  4 Dark Blue Flat Stem No. 2
  5 Dark Blue Flat Stem No. 3
  6 Dark Blue Flat Stem No. 4
  7 Light Blue Web No. 1
  8 Light Blue Web No. 2
  9 Eggshell Diagonal Mosaic No. 1
  10 Eggshell Diagonal Mosaic No. 2
  11 Light Blue Scotch No. 1
  12 Light Blue Scotch No. 2
  13 Light Blue Mosaic No. 1
  14 Light Blue Mosaic No. 2

  15 Dark Blue Flat Stem No. 1
  16 Dark Blue Flat Stem No. 2
  17 Dark Blue Flat Stem No. 3
  18 Dark Blue Flat Stem No. 4

Latchet and Rya Colors:

  1 and 2   Gold Rya
  3, 4, 5, and 6   Dark Blue Rya
  7 and 8   Light Blue Rya
  9 and 10   Yellow Latchet
  11, 12, 13, and 14   Medium Gold Latchet
  15, 16, 17, and 18   Dark Gold and Rust Latchet

201

A Directory
of Flat Stitches

The following stitch diagrams will lead you step by step through each of the flat needlepoint stitches employed in this book. The parallel horizontal and vertical threads represent the parallel threads of the rug canvas. The heavy black lines with the numbers at each end represent the stitches. In all cases, bring the needle up through the canvas through hole number one. Go back down through the canvas at hole number two. Continue the stitches, coming up through the canvas at each subsequent odd number and going back down through the canvas at each subsequent even number.

Continental No. 1

FIG. 173

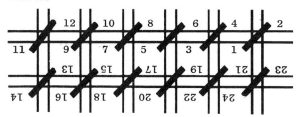

Continental No. 2

FIG. 174

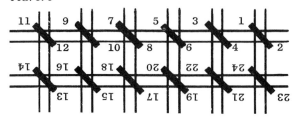

Diagonal Mosaic No. 1

FIG. 175

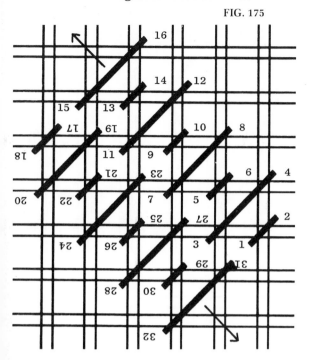

Diagonal Mosaic No. 2

FIG. 176

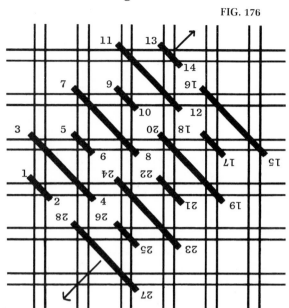

Scotch No. 1

FIG. 177

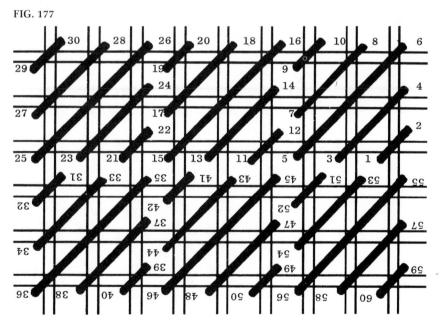

203

Scotch No. 2
FIG. 178

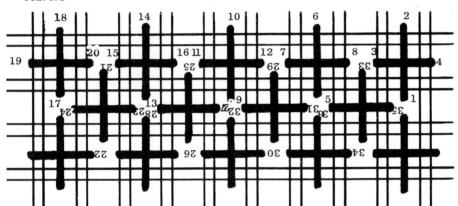

Straight Cross
FIG. 179

Milanese
FIG. 180

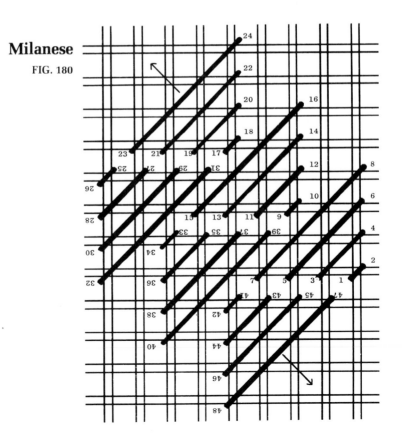

Milanese

FIG. 181

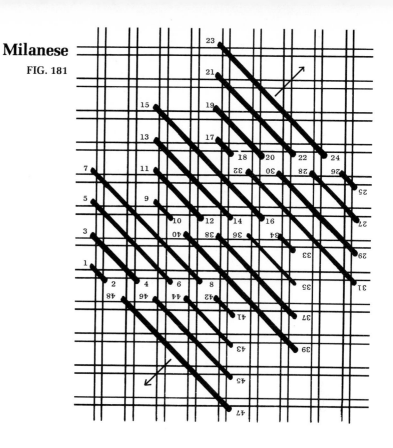

Flat Stem No. 1

FIG. 182

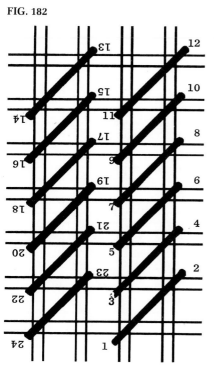

Flat Stem No. 2

FIG. 183

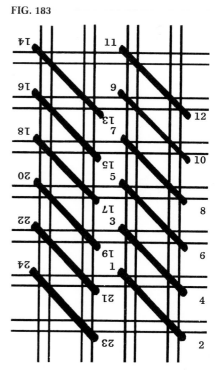

Flat Stem No. 3 ,

FIG. 184

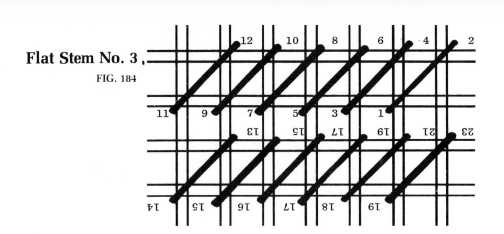

Flat Stem No. 4

FIG. 185

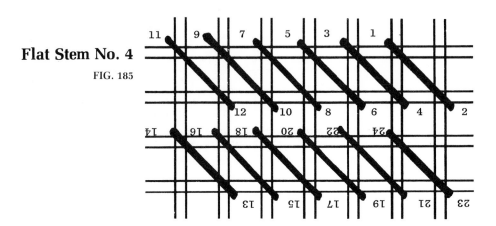

Flat Stem No. 5

FIG. 186

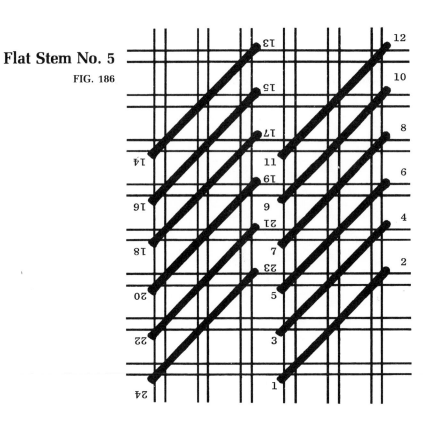

206

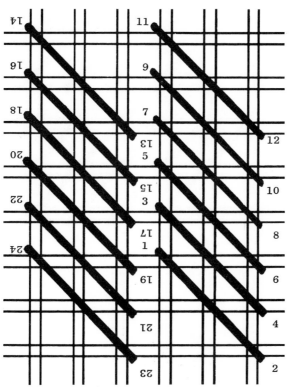

Flat Stem No. 6

FIG. 187

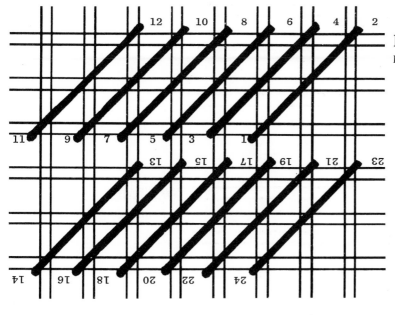

Flat Stem No. 7

FIG. 188

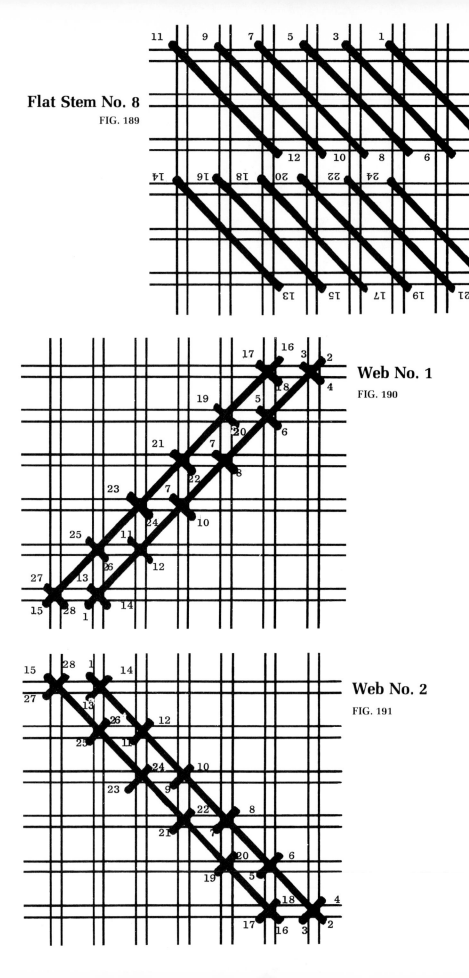

Flat Stem No. 8
FIG. 189

Web No. 1
FIG. 190

Web No. 2
FIG. 191

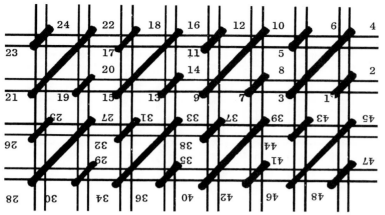

Mosaic No. 1
FIG. 192

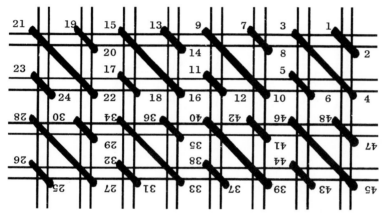

Mosaic No. 2
FIG. 193

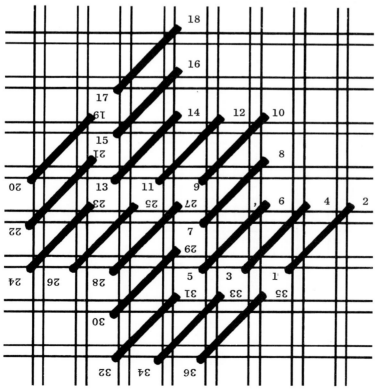

Byzantine No. 1
FIG. 194

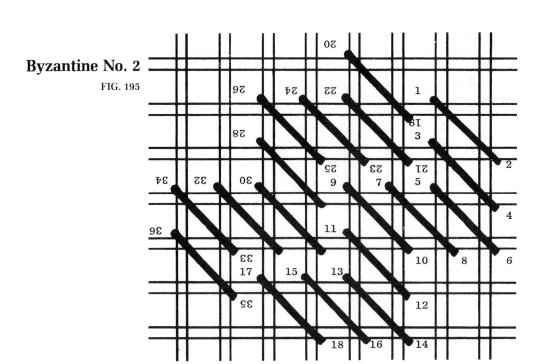

Byzantine No. 3

FIG. 196

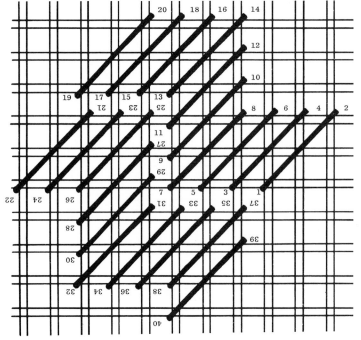

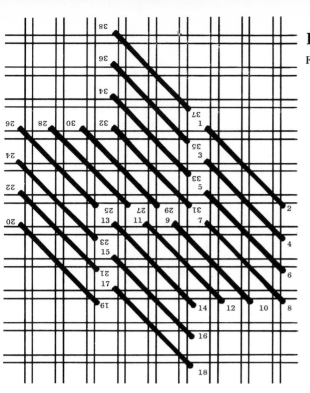

Byzantine No. 4
FIG. 197

Vertical Satin
FIG. 198

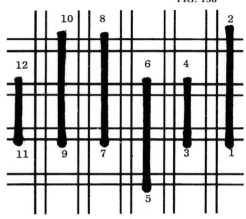

Horizontal Satin
FIG. 199

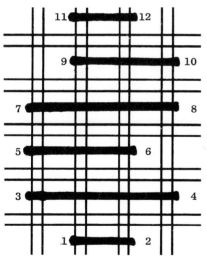

Diagonal Satin
FIG. 200

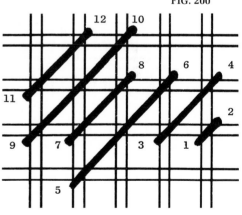

Diagonal Satin
FIG. 201

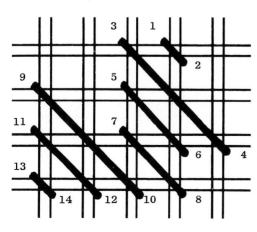

211

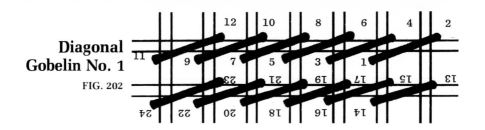

Diagonal Gobelin No. 1

FIG. 202

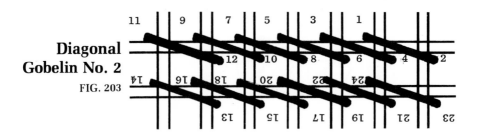

Diagonal Gobelin No. 2

FIG. 203

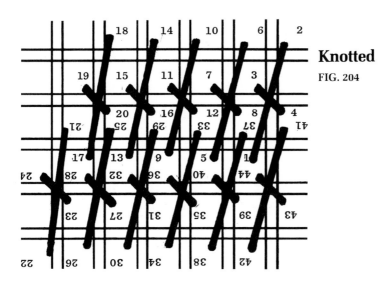

Knotted

FIG. 204

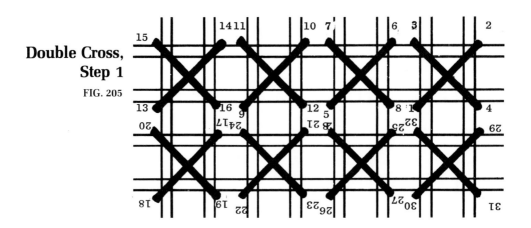

Double Cross, Step 1

FIG. 205

Double Cross, Step 2

FIG. 206

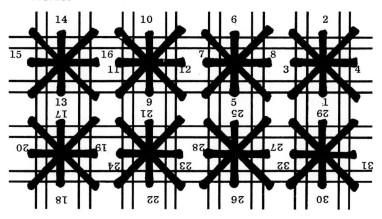

Leaf

FIG. 207

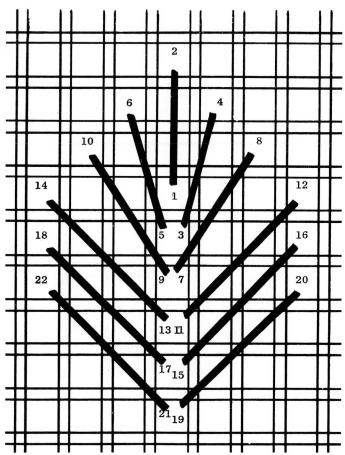

KEYED DIAGRAMS FOR COLOR SECTION

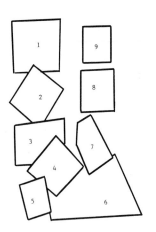

COLOR PLATE 1
1—Giant Sunflower, Figs. 19 and 20
2—Indian Motif Number Four, Figs. 84,
    85, and 86
3—Aztec Motif, Figs. 40 and 41
4—Grid Design, Figs. 125 and 126
5—Tile Number Six, Figs. 159 and 160
6 and 7—Aztec Priest, Figs. 82 and 83
8—Indian Motif Number Three, Figs. 78 and 79
9—Indian Tree Motif, Figs. 87 and 88

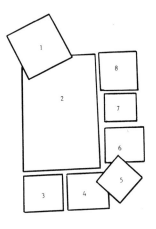

COLOR PLATE 2
1—Shields, Figs. 93 and 94
2, 3, and 4—Tree of Life Quilt Design,
    Figs. 72 and 73
5 and 7—Blazing Star Quilt Design,
    Figs. 157 and 158
6—Flying Geese Quilt Design, Figs. 74 and 75
8—Stained Glass, Figs. 76 and 77

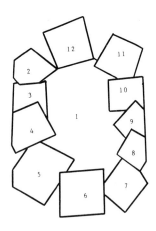

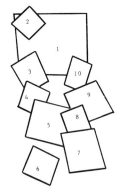

COLOR PLATE 3
1—Paisley Rug, Figs. 141, 142, and 143
2—Indian Motif Number 4, Figs. 84, 85, and 86
3—Interlocking Bands, Figs. 34 and 35
4—Giant Flower, Figs. 66 and 67
5 and 10—Byzantine Spires, Figs. 31, 32, and 33
6—Modern Paisley, Figs. 52 and 53
7—Graphic V, Figs. 117 and 118
8—Small Flowers, Figs. 131 and 132
9—Graphic Double V, Figs. 121 and 122
11—Flowers and Stripes, Figs. 135 and 136
12—Waves, Figs. 127 and 128

COLOR PLATE 4
1—Small Butterfly, Figs. 99 and 100 and
    Flowers and Stripes, Figs. 135 and 136
2—Sailboat, Figs. 113 and 114
3—Czech Girl, Figs. 107 and 108
4 and 9—Four-petaled Flower, Figs. 171 and 17
5—Whimsical Lion, Figs. 109 and 110
6—Small Butterfly, Figs. 99 and 100
7—Owl with Flowers, Figs. 101 and 102
8—Anchor and Stars, Figs. 115 and 116
10—Scattered Mushrooms, Figs. 105 and 106

COLOR PLATE 5
1—Graphic V, Figs. 117 and 118
2—Giant Butterfly, Figs. 137 and 138
3—Daisies, Figs. 139 and 140
4—Key on Broken Cane, Figs. 97 and 98
5—Pennsylvania Dutch Tulips, Figs. 50 and 51
6—Rose on Broken Cane, Figs. 148, 149, and 150
7—Shields, Figs. 93 and 94
8—Tile Number One, Figs. 21 and 22

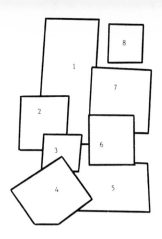

COLOR PLATE 6
1—Byzantine Square, Figs. 42 and 43
2—Nordic Sunburst, Figs. 48 and 49
3—Tile Number Four, Figs. 133 and 134
4—Small Flowers, Figs. 131 and 132
5—Indian Motif Number One, Figs. 54 and 55
6—Bamboo with Tassels, Figs. 153 and 154
7—Indian Motif Number Two, Figs. 58 and 59
8—Chinese Medallion, Figs. 27 and 28
9—Bamboo Fan, Figs. 151 and 152

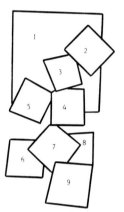

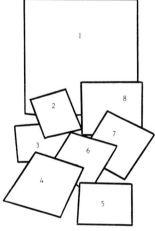
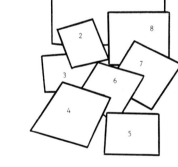

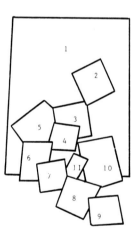

COLOR PLATE 7
1—Blazing Star Quilt Design,
   Figs. 157 and 158
2—Small Sunflowers, Figs. 165 and 166
3—Giant Sunflower, Figs. 19 and 20
4—Pennsylvania Dutch Tulips,
   Figs. 50 and 51
5—Byzantine Square, Figs. 42 and 43
6—Grid Design, Figs. 125 and 126
7—Scroll Flowers, Figs. 44 and 45
8—Heraldic Eagle, Figs. 91 and 92

COLOR PLATE 8
1 and 9—Tile Number Three, Figs. 38 and 39
2—Giant Milanese, Figs. 29 and 30
3—Leaf Stitch Center, Figs. 46 and 47
4—Bee, Figs. 144 and 145
5—Stained Glass, Figs. 76 and 77
6—Paisley with Border, Figs. 64 and 65
7—Stepping Stones Quilt Design,
   Figs. 68 and 69
8—Diamonds and Crosses, Figs. 36 and 37
10—Florentine Tile, Figs. 95 and 96
11—Small Paisley, Figs. 62 and 63

215

Suppliers

Most of the materials used for the projects in this book are readily available at needlecraft shops or the art needlework department of large department stores. In addition, the following manufacturers and retail stores carry most of the supplies required by this book.

Emil Bernat & Sons, 230 Fifth Avenue, New York, N.Y. 10001
Coats and Clark, 430 Park Avenue, New York, N.Y. 10022
Columbia-Minerva Corp., 295 Fifth Avenue, New York, N.Y. 10010
D.M.C. Corp., 107 Trumbull Street, Elizabeth, N.J. 07206
Design Point Needlepoint, 15 Christopher Street, New York, N.Y. 10014
Dritz, Scovill Mfg. Corp., 350 Fifth Avenue, New York, N.Y. 10001
Fibre Yarn, 840 Sixth Avenue, New York, N.Y. 10001
Minuet, 230 Fifth Avenue, New York, N.Y. 10001
Paternayan Brothers, 312 East 95th Street, New York, N.Y. 10028
The Stitchery, Wellesley, Mass. 02181
Joan Toggitt, Ltd., 246 Fifth Avenue, New York, N.Y. 10001
Bernhard Ulmann Co., 30-20 Thomson Avenue, Long Island City, N.Y. 11101
Woolcraft, Ltd., Alice Godkin, #4 Trading Company Building, Regina, Sask., Canada

If you should have difficulty finding special materials, please contact the authors in care of their publishers, Crown Publishers, Inc., One Park Avenue, New York, N.Y. 10016, enclosing a stamped, self-addressed envelope, for more information.

Index